THE WORLD'S GREATEST-EVER
CURRIES

THE WORLD'S GREATEST-EVER
CURRIES

THE 150 BEST-LOVED HOT AND SPICY DISHES MADE SIMPLE

Mridula Baljekar

HERMES HOUSE

Above: *Numerous varieties of beans, peas and lentils are on sale in this pulse shop, along with spice mixes for cooking them.*

famous for its forts and palaces, and for its unique cuisine. Mogul traditions are strong here: even though the state has never been ruled by the Muslim rulers, the last Mogul emperor retired to the capital city Hyderabad, causing a culinary revolution that influenced the whole region. Kababs, biryanis and kormas exist side by side with hot, fiery local foods and a wide variety of rice, which is grown locally.

West India

In western India lies the state of Gujarat. Most Gujaratis are strictly vegetarian and, unlike the many non-meat eaters in India who eat fish, they eat neither fish nor eggs. Their religion emphasizes the respect that must be shown to all living beings, and prohibits the taking of any life for reasons of personal enjoyment. As a result, the Gujaratis have truly perfected the art of vegetarian cooking. Fresh vegetables, lentils, beans, peas and dairy products have taken centre stage, and dairy products are abundant. People take yogurt and buttermilk on a daily basis, and use them in cooking. Breads

are skilfully made, using both millet flour and maize flour (cornmeal).

The most famous culinary export of Gujarat is the vegetable- and lentil-based dhansak. About 13 centuries ago, a group of Persians fled their country to avoid religious persecution. Gujarat, being open to the sea, was the most convenient point from which to enter India. The Persians were made to feel

at home here, and became known as the Parsis. They adapted the rich and varied culture of Gujarat and eventually spread further west, to Bombay.

Bombay is situated on the edge of the deep blue Arabian Sea, and it is here that the Gateway of India was built during the British Raj, to commemorate a visit by the Prince of Wales. Bombay is the capital of Maharashtra, a mainly vegetarian state with a cosmopolitan population that has given rise to a rich and varied cuisine. Bombay is probably the only city in India where food from almost any part of the country can be sampled. As well as Indian food, Chinese dishes with an Indian twist can be found in the numerous restaurants throughout this vibrant city. Fresh fish and shellfish are also plentiful in the area.

To the south of Bombay is Goa, where the lure of Indian spices brought Portuguese traders, who colonized the area. Goa remained under Portuguese rule until 1962, and the influence the Portuguese left behind has created a happy marriage between East and West. Goa's most famous export is vindaloo, which has Portuguese origins.

Below: *Fisherman inspect their early morning catch on the beaches of Kerala.*

PRINCIPLES of INDIAN COOKING

Until recently, no written record of Indian recipes has existed in India itself. Recipes have traditionally been handed down from one generation to another. Far from being a disadvantage, this has actually helped to fire the imagination of the creative cook, and many dishes that first started out as experiments in spice blends and flavour combinations have now become world classics.

Spices and aromatics

The key to successful Indian cooking lies in the art of blending spices and herbs, rather than sophisticated cooking techniques. The traditional Indian cook relies on instinct rather than written recipes when measuring and combining spices, and in this way unique and very personal tastes can be created. This is one reason why the same dish from one region can look and taste quite different, according to who has cooked it.

Herbs are added to a dish during the cooking time to add flavour and aroma, but spices, including those used mainly for taste or for aroma, perform a more complex role.

Spices can be divided into two main groups: those that are integrated into a dish by the end of the cooking process, and those that are removed. The spices in the first group add taste, texture and colour. Different combinations are used, and no single spice is allowed to dominate the final flavour. Useful spices in this group include coriander, cumin, turmeric and garam masala, all in ground form.

The second group of spices add aroma to a dish. They remain identifiable at the end of cooking, as most of them are used whole. Once these spices have released their aroma, their function is complete and they are not eaten, but removed from the dish before serving or simply left on one side of the plate. Examples of this type of spice are whole cloves, cardamom pods, cinnamon sticks and bay leaves. These spices can also be ground, in which case they will blend into the sauce during cooking, and will be eaten in the dish in the same way as any other ground spice.

Adding flavour

Having chosen which spices to use, you can then decide what kind of flavours you would like to create. For instance, dry-roasting and grinding flavouring ingredients before adding them to a dish creates a completely different taste and aroma from frying the raw ground spices in hot fat before adding the main ingredients. The flavour of a dish will also vary according to the sequence in which the spices are added, and the length of time each spice is fried and allowed to release its flavour.

Indian cooking lends itself to being personalized by different cooks, and with even just two or three spices, you can create distinctly varied dishes.

Below: Spices and seasonings are what gives Indian food its unique character.

What is a curry?

In India, the word curry refers to a sauce or gravy used as an accompaniment to moisten grains of *chawal* (rice) or to make *rotis* (bread) more enjoyable. The rice or bread are considered the main dish of the meal.

The word curry is generally believed to be an anglicized version of the south Indian word *kaari*. It belongs to the Tamil language, which is spoken in the state of Tamil Nadu, of which Madras is the capital. In Tamil, the word means sauce and it is thought that when the British were active in this area, the spelling was somehow changed to curry. Other theories suggest that the word *cury* has existed in English in the context of cooking since the 14th century, and that it was originally derived from the French verb *cuire* (to cook).

The main ingredients of a curry can vary enormously, and two highly dissimilar dishes can be equally deserving of the name. Even the lentil dish known as *dhal*, which bears no resemblance to a sauce, falls under the definition of a curry; in India, *dhal-chawal* and *dhal-roti* are eaten on a daily basis.

A vegetable curry usually consists of a selection of fresh vegetables cooked in a sauce, which can have a thick or a thin consistency, depending on the style of cooking in the region. The sauces for meat, poultry and fish curries also vary in consistency, and are all designed to be served with rice or bread. Gujarat in the west and Punjab in the north also make spiced curries using just yogurt mixed with a little *besan* (gram flour). Made without meat, poultry or vegetables, these dishes are known as *khadis*.

Above: Most of the key ingredients needed for Indian curries are now available from large supermarkets, but Indian food stores will usually stock a wider selection.

What to eat with a curry

In south and eastern India, curries are always served with rice, which, as the region's main crop, is the staple food of the area, and is eaten daily. Wheat grows abundantly in north India, and in most northern regions, breads such as naan, chapatis and parathas are eaten with curries and with dry, spiced vegetable and lentil dishes. In the Punjab region, however, breads made from *besan* and *makki* (cornmeal) are more usually served with curries. In western India, curries are eaten with breads made with flour prepared from *jowar* (millet) and *bajra* (milo).

Below: Fresh coriander

Freezing fresh coriander

Fresh coriander (cilantro) is widely used in Indian cooking. Its flavour and aroma make it an important ingredient, and the fresh leaves make a attractive garnish. Buy bunches of coriander and freeze what is not required immediately.

1 Cut off the roots and any thick stalks, retaining the fine stalks.

2 Wash the leaves in cold water and leave in a strainer to drain.

3 When the leaves are dry, chop them finely and store them in small quantities in plastic bags or airtight containers in the freezer.

Coriander

There is no substitute for fresh coriander (cilantro), and the more that is used in Indian cooking the better. Coriander imparts a wonderful aroma and flavour, and is used both as an ingredient in cooking, and sprinkled over dishes as a garnish. Chopped coriander can be frozen successfully; the frozen coriander does not need to be defrosted before use. Coriander seeds and ground coriander powder are used for flavouring. The seeds have a pungent, slightly lemony flavour, and are used coarsely ground in meat, fish and poultry dishes. Ground coriander, a brownish powder, is an important constituent of any curry spice mixture.

Mint

There are many varieties of mint available, and the stronger-flavoured types tend to be used in Indian cooking. These taste slightly sweet and have a cool aftertaste. Mint has a fresh, stimulating aroma and is traditionally used with lamb, as well as for flavouring some vegetables, and for making chutneys and refreshing raitas. Mint is added at the end of cooking time, in order to retain the flavour.

Fenugreek

Fresh fenugreek is generally sold in bunches. It has very small leaves and is used to flavour meat and vegetarian dishes. Always discard the stalks, which will impart an unpleasant bitterness to a dish if used. Fenugreek seeds are flat, extremely pungent and slightly bitter. They only appear in a few recipes, where they are added whole, mainly for taste; these should be used cautiously. Dried fenugreek leaves are sold in Indian food stores. Store them in an airtight jar, in a cool, dark place; they will keep for about 12 months. Fenugreek seeds are small and pungent, and are widely used in spice mixtures.

Below: Aromatic fresh fenugreek leaves are widely used in savoury Indian dishes.

CURRY POWDERS and PASTES

Powders and pastes are blends of spices, chillies and herbs that are used as the basis of a curry. Traditional Indian households would blend individual spices as needed, but for convenience you may prefer to prepare a quantity in advance.

Curry powder

This is a basic recipe for a dry spice blend for use in any curry dish. It is a mild recipe, but you could increase the quantity of dried chilli for a hotter taste.

MAKES ABOUT 115G/4OZ/½ CUP

50g/2oz/½ cup coriander seeds
60ml/4 tbsp cumin seeds
30ml/2 tbsp fennel seeds
30ml/2 tbsp fenugreek seeds
4 dried red chillies
5 curry leaves
15ml/1 tbsp chilli powder
15ml/1 tbsp ground turmeric
2.5ml/½ tsp salt

1 Dry-roast the whole spices in a wok, karahi or large pan for 8–10 minutes, shaking the pan until the spices darken and release a rich aroma. Allow to cool.

2 Put the dry-roasted whole spices in a spice mill and grind to a fine powder.

3 Add the ground, roasted spices to the chilli powder, turmeric and salt in a large glass bowl and mix well. Store the curry powder in an airtight container.

Garam masala

Garam means hot and masala means spices, and this mixture uses spices that are known to heat the body, such as black peppercorns and cloves. Garam masala is used mainly for meat, although it can be used in poultry and rice dishes. The aroma is generally considered too strong for fish or vegetable dishes.

MAKES ABOUT 50G/2OZ/¼ CUP

10 dried red chillies
3 × 2.5cm/1in pieces cinnamon stick
2 curry leaves
30ml/2 tbsp coriander seeds
30ml/2 tbsp cumin seeds
5ml/1 tsp black peppercorns
5ml/1 tsp cloves
5ml/1 tsp fenugreek seeds
5ml/1 tsp black mustard seeds
1.5ml/¼ tsp chilli powder

1 Dry-roast the whole dried red chillies, cinnamon sticks and curry leaves in a wok, karahi or large pan over a low heat for about 2 minutes.

2 Add the coriander and cumin seeds, black peppercorns, cloves, fenugreek and mustard seeds, and dry-roast for 8–10 minutes, shaking the pan from side to side until the spices begin to darken in colour and release a rich aroma. Allow the mixture to cool.

3 Using either a spice mill or a stainless steel mortar and pestle, grind the roasted spices to a fine powder.

4 Transfer the powder to a glass bowl and mix in the chilli powder. Store in an airtight container.

COOK'S TIP

Both the curry powder and the garam masala will keep for 2–4 months in an airtight container in a cool, dark place. Once opened, store in the refrigerator.

VARIATIONS

For convenience, you can buy garam masala ready-made, or try any of the following pastes in alternative flavours:
• Tandoori masala
• Kashmiri masala
• Madras masala
• Sambhar masala
• Dhansak masala
• Green masala

BREADS

Breads are an integral part of any Indian meal. Most traditional Indian breads are unleavened, that is, made without any raising agent, and are made with wholemeal (whole-wheat) flour, known as chapati flour or atta.

Throughout India, breads vary from region to region, depending on local ingredients. Some breads are cooked dry on a hot griddle, while some are fried with a little oil, and others are deep-fried to make small savoury puffs. To enjoy Indian breads at their best they should be made just before you are ready to serve the meal, so that they can be eaten hot.

Naan

Probably the most well-known Indian bread outside India is naan, from the north of the country. Naan is made with plain (all-purpose) flour, yogurt and yeast; some contemporary recipes favour the use of a chemical raising agent such as bicarbonate of soda (baking soda) or self-raising (self-rising) flour as a leaven in place of yeast. The yogurt is important for the fermentation of the dough, and some naan are made entirely using a yogurt fermentation. Fermentation gives the bread its characteristic light, puffy texture and soft crust. The flavour comes partly from the soured yogurt and partly from the *tandoor*, which is the the clay oven, sunk into the ground, in which the bread is traditionally cooked. The bread is flattened against the blisteringly hot walls of the oven and the pull of gravity produces the characteristic teardrop shape. As the dough scorches and puffs up, it produces a bread that is soft and crisp. Naan can be eaten with almost any meat or vegetable dish. There are many types of flavoured naan sold commercially, including plain, coriander (cilantro) and garlic, and masala naan.

Chapatis

The favourite bread of central and southern India is the chapati, a thin, flat, unleavened bread made from ground

Above: Chapatis and parathas

Below: Poppadums

wholemeal flour. Chapatis are cooked on a hot *tava*, a concave-shaped Indian griddle. Chapatis have a light texture and fairly bland flavour, which makes them an ideal accompaniment for highly spiced curry dishes. Spices can be added to the flour to give more flavour.

Rotis

There are many variations of chapatis, including *rotis* and *dana rotis*. These are unleavened breads, made using chapati flour to which ghee, oil, celery seeds and/or fresh coriander are added. They are rolled out thinly and cooked like chapatis.

Parathas

A paratha is similar to a chapati except that it contains ghee (clarified butter), which gives the bread a richer flavour and flakier texture. Parathas are much thicker than chapatis and are shallow-fried. Plain parathas are often eaten for lunch, and they go well with most vegetable dishes. They can be stuffed with various fillings, the most popular being spiced potato. Stuffed parathas are served as a snack.

Pooris

Another popular variation on the chapati is the poori, which is a small, deep-fried puffy bread made from chapati flour. Pooris are best eaten sizzling hot and are traditionally served for breakfast. They can be plain or flavoured with spices, such as cumin, turmeric and chilli powder, which are mixed into the dough. Pooris are often served with fish or vegetable curries.

Poppadums

These are now widely available outside of India. These are large, thin crisp disks, which can be bought ready-cooked or ready-to-cook. In India they are served with vegetarian meals. They are sold in markets and by street vendors, and are available plain or flavoured with spices or seasoned with ground red or black pepper. The dough is generally made from dried beans, but can also be made from potatoes or sago. It is thinly rolled and left to dry in the sun. Poppadums are cooked either by deep-frying or placing under a hot grill (broiler).

Above: Naan

EQUIPMENT and UTENSILS

While a reasonably stocked kitchen will provide most of the equipment needed for cooking Indian curries, it may still be necessary to invest in one or two more specialist items to ensure perfect results.

Chapati griddle

Known in India as a *tava*, the chapati griddle allows chapatis and other breads to be cooked without burning. The heavy wrought-iron frying pan can also be used to dry-roast spices. Traditionally, the griddle would be set over an open fire but it will work equally well on a gas flame or electric hob.

Chapati rolling board

This round wooden board on short stubby legs is used to mould breads into shape; the extra height provided by the legs helps to disperse excess dry flour. A wooden pastry board makes an appropriate substitute.

Chapati rolling pin

The traditional chapati rolling pin is thinner in shape than Western rolling pins, and comes in many different sizes. Use whichever size feels the most comfortable in your hands.

Heat diffuser

Many curries are left to simmer slowly over a low heat, and a heat diffuser will help to prevent burning on the base of the karahi or wok.

Grinding stone and pin

The traditional oblong grinding stone is the Indian equivalent of the Western food processor. Fresh and dry ingredients are placed on the heavy slate stone, which is marked with notches to hold ingredients in place. The ingredients are then pulverized against the stone, using the heavy rolling pin.

Table sizzler

This heated appliance allows food that is still cooking to be brought to the dinner table ready for serving. It is very useful for entertaining.

Slotted spoon

Stirring cooked, drained rice with a slotted spoon will make the rice soft, fluffy by allowing air in between the grains; the slots in the spoon prevent the grains from breaking as the rice is moved around the pan. The spoon also used to remove foods from hot oil or other cooking liquids.

Chapati spoon

The square, flat-headed chapati spoon is used for turning roasting breads on the hot chapati griddle. A fish slice (spatula) may also be used.

Spice mill

An electric spice mill is useful for grinding small quantities of

Above: Chapati griddle and chapati rolling pin

Left: Grinding stone and rolling pin, tongs and stainless steel mortar and pestle

Below right: Heat diffuser

Below:
A traditional cast-iron karahi

Karahi

Basically an Indian frying pan, the karahi, is similar to a wok but is more rounded in shape and is made of heavier metal: originally, the karahi would be made of cast iron, although a variety of metals are now used. Karahis are available in various sizes, including small ones for cooking single portions. Serving food from a karahi at the table adds an authentic touch to the meal.

Wok

This is a good substitute for a karahi for cooking most types of Indian dish. Buy the appropriate wok for your cooker. Round-bottomed woks can be used on gas hobs only; flat-bottomed woks are for use on electric hobs.

Stainless steel pans

Quality kitchen pans in various sizes are essential for cooking rice, vegetables and other ingredients. A heavy-based non-stick frying pan can be used in place of a karahi or wok.

Above: Stainless steel pans

ingredients such as spices. A coffee grinder – used solely for this purpose, as it will retain the strong smell of the spices – would make a good substitute.

Stainless steel mortar and pestle

These are ideal for grinding small amounts of wet ingredients, such as fresh root ginger, chillies and garlic. Stainless steel is everlasting and will not retain the strong flavours of the spices.

Stone mortar and pestle

A heavy granite mortar and pestle is traditionally used to grind small amounts of ingredients, both wet and dry.

Pastry brush

Use for brushing and basting meats and vegetables lightly with oil before and during grilling (broiling).

Balloon whisk

A metal whisk is useful for beating yogurt and dairy or coconut cream before adding to recipes.

Knives

Kitchen knives in a range of sizes are essential. Keep knives sharp to make it easier to chop ingredients and to ensure neat edges when cutting.

Colander and sieve

Use for draining boiled rice and vegetables, and for straining ingredients. Choose a long-handled, sturdy colander and sieve made from stainless steel, as these allow you to stand back to pour steaming rice out of a pan, and will not discolour like plastic ones.

Food processor

This is essential for blending the ingredients. Smaller quantities can be ground in a mortar and pestle.

Right: From left, stainless steel colander and sieve

NORTH INDIA

The cuisine of northern India has been heavily influenced by a great many foreign settlers, traders and pilgrims. The most notable of these were the Moguls, who added Mughlai food and a selection of exotic fruit and nuts to the established traditions of Kashmir and Punjab.

KASHMIRI CHICKEN CURRY

Surrounded by the snow-capped Himalayas, Kashmir is popularly known as the "Switzerland of the East". The state is also renowned for its rich culinary heritage, and this aromatic dish is one of the simplest among the region's repertoire.

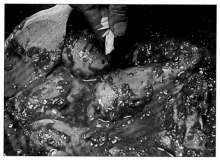

2 Rub the chicken pieces with the marinade and allow to rest in a cool place for a further 2 hours, or in the refrigerator overnight. Bring to room temperature before cooking.

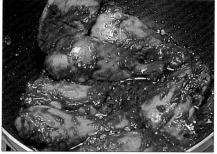

3 Heat the oil in a wok, karahi or large pan and fry half the ginger and all the garlic until golden. Add the chicken and fry until both sides are sealed. Cover and cook until the chicken is tender, and the oil has separated from the sauce.

SERVES 4–6

20ml/4 tsp Kashmiri masala paste
60ml/4 tbsp tomato ketchup
5ml/1 tsp Worcestershire sauce
5ml/1 tsp five-spice powder
5ml/1 tsp granulated sugar
8 chicken joints, skinned
45ml/3 tbsp vegetable oil
5cm/2in piece fresh root ginger, finely
    shredded
4 garlic cloves, crushed
juice of 1 lemon
15ml/1 tbsp coriander (cilantro) leaves,
    finely chopped
salt

1 To make the marinade, mix the masala paste, tomato ketchup, Worcestershire sauce, five-spice powder, salt and sugar. Allow the mixture to rest in a warm place until the sugar has dissolved.

4 Sprinkle the chicken with the lemon juice, remaining ginger and chopped coriander leaves, and mix in well. Serve hot. Plain boiled rice would make a good accompaniment.

TANDOORI CHICKEN

Punjab, in northern India, is the home of tandoori food. The tandoor, or clay oven, originated in Egypt and found its way into India with the Moguls. It is probably the most versatile oven in the world, capable of roasting, grilling and baking all at the same time.

SERVES 4–6

1.3kg/3lb oven-ready chicken
250ml/8fl oz/1 cup natural (plain)
   yogurt, beaten
60ml/4 tbsp tandoori masala paste
75g/3oz/2 tbsp ghee or vegetable oil
salt
lemon slice and onion rings, to garnish
lettuce, to serve

1 Using a small, sharp knife or scissors, remove the skin from the chicken and trim off any excess fat. Using a fork, prick the flesh at random.

2 Cut the chicken in half down the centre and through the breast. Cut each piece in half again. Make a few deep gashes diagonally into the flesh.

3 Mix the yogurt with the masala paste and season with salt. Spread the chicken with the yogurt mixture, spreading some into the gashes. Leave to marinate in a cool place for at least 2 hours, or in the refrigerator overnight.

4 Preheat the oven to 240°C/475°F/ Gas 9. Place the chicken quarters on a wire rack in a deep baking tray. Spread the chicken with any excess marinade, reserving a little for basting halfway through the cooking time.

COOK'S TIP
If the chicken is left overnight in the refrigerator, remove it a hour or two before you want to start cooking to allow it to return to room temperature.

5 Melt the ghee and pour over the chicken pieces to seal the surface. This helps to keep the centre moist during roasting. Roast the chicken for about 10 minutes, then remove from the oven, leaving the oven on.

6 Baste the chicken with the remaining marinade. Return to the oven and switch off the heat. Leave the chicken in the oven for 15–20 minutes without opening the door. Serve on a bed of lettuce and garnish with the lemon and onion rings.

KARAHI CHICKEN with MINT

A karahi is similar to a Chinese wok, and its use is most widespread in northern India, which is closest to the border with China. A traditional karahi is made of heavy cast iron, which is excellent for heat distribution and retention, and it is used extensively for cooking all types of meat, poultry and vegetable dishes. Because of its shape, it is also ideal for deep-frying and is used for this purpose all over India.

2 Heat the oil in a large pan, add the chopped spring onions and stir-fry for about 2 minutes until soft.

3 Add the boiled chicken strips to the pan and stir-fry briskly over a medium heat for about 3 minutes, or until the chicken is browned.

SERVES 4

450g/1lb chicken breast fillets, skinned and
   cut into strips
300ml/½ pint/1¼ cups water
30ml/2 tbsp vegetable oil
2 small bunches spring onions
   (scallions), roughly chopped
5ml/1 tsp grated fresh root ginger
5ml/1 tsp crushed dried red chilli
30ml/2 tbsp lemon juice
30ml/2 tbsp chopped fresh coriander
   (cilantro), plus extra sprigs to garnish
30ml/2 tbsp chopped fresh mint, plus extra
   sprigs to garnish
3 tomatoes, seeded and roughly chopped
5ml/1 tsp salt

1 Put the chicken and water into a large pan, bring to the boil and lower the heat to medium. Cook for about 10 minutes or until the water has evaporated and the chicken is cooked. Remove the pan from the heat and set aside.

4 Add the grated fresh root ginger, chilli, lemon juice, chopped coriander and mint, tomatoes and salt, and stir gently to blend the flavours.

5 Transfer the curry to a warmed serving platter and garnish with fresh coriander and mint sprigs before serving. Plain boiled rice would make a good accompaniment to this dish.

VARIATION

Use strips of turkey breast meat or pork tenderloin instead of chicken. If using, pork tenderloin, flatten the meat with a steak mallet first to tenderize it, then cut into strips and use as directed.

KARAHI CHICKEN with FRESH FENUGREEK

This karahi chicken was the dish that inspired a style of cooking known as karahi cuisine in northern India, where fenugreek is a typical flavouring agent. In the West, dried fenugreek leaves can be used for convenience, as fresh fenugreek is generally more difficult to find. The dried leaves are sold in Indian and Pakistani food stores throughout the year, and will keep well in an airtight jar.

SERVES 4

225g/8oz chicken thigh meat, skinned
   and cut into strips
225g/8oz chicken breast fillets, skinned
   and cut into strips
2.5ml/½ tsp crushed garlic
5ml/1 tsp chilli powder
2.5ml/½ tsp salt
10ml/2 tsp tomato purée (paste)
30ml/2 tbsp vegetable oil
1 bunch fresh fenugreek leaves or
   15ml/1 tbsp dried
15ml/1 tbsp chopped fresh coriander
   (cilantro)

1 Bring a large pan of water to the boil, add the chicken strips and cook for 5–7 minutes. Drain and set aside.

2 In a bowl, combine the garlic, chilli powder and salt with the tomato purée.

COOK'S TIP
Discard the stems of fresh fenugreek, as they will impart a bitter flavour to the dish.

3 Heat the oil in a wok, karahi or large pan. Lower the heat and add the tomato purée and spice mixture.

4 Add the chicken pieces and stir-fry for 5–7 minutes. Lower the heat further.

5 Add the fenugreek leaves and the chopped fresh coriander to the pan. Continue to stir-fry for 5–7 minutes, then pour in 300ml/½ pint/1¼ cups water, cover and cook for a further 5 minutes. Serve hot.

CHICKEN TIKKA MASALA

Though chicken tikka is a traditional dish from northern India, masala *is pure invention. The word refers to the sauce in which the cooked tikka is simmered and which is a western adaptation. However, it is not dissimilar to another traditional Indian dish known as butter chicken, in which cooked tandoori chicken is simmered in a creamy sauce.*

SERVES 4

675g/1½lb chicken breast fillets, skinned
90ml/6 tbsp tikka paste
60ml/4 tbsp natural (plain) yogurt
30ml/2 tbsp vegetable oil
1 onion, chopped
1 garlic clove, crushed
1 fresh green chilli, seeded and chopped
2.5cm/1in piece fresh root ginger, grated
15ml/1 tbsp tomato purée (paste)
15ml/1 tbsp ground almonds
250ml/8fl oz/1 cup water
45ml/3 tbsp ghee or butter, melted
50ml/2fl oz/¼ cup double (heavy) cream
15ml/1 tbsp lemon juice
fresh coriander (cilantro) sprigs, natural
    (plain) yogurt and toasted cumin seeds
    to garnish
naan bread, to serve

1 Cut the chicken into 2.5cm/1in cubes. Put half of the tikka paste and the yogurt into a bowl, then stir in the chicken. Leave to marinate for 20 minutes.

COOK'S TIP
Soak wooden kebab skewers in water before use to prevent them from burning while under the grill (broiler).

2 For the tikka sauce, heat the oil and fry the onion, garlic, chilli and ginger for 5 minutes. Add the remaining tikka paste and fry for 2 minutes. Add the tomato purée, almonds and water, and simmer for 15 minutes.

3 Thread the chicken on to wooden kebab skewers. Preheat the grill (broiler).

4 Brush the chicken pieces with the melted butter and grill (broil) under a medium heat for about 15 minutes. Occasionally, turn and brush the chicken pieces with more butter.

5 Put the tikka sauce in a blender or food processor and process until smooth. Return the sauce to the pan and stir in the cream and lemon juice.

6 Remove the chicken from the grill, slide the cubes off the wooden skewers and add them to the pan. Simmer gently for 5 minutes more. Garnish with fresh coriander, yogurt and cumin seeds, and serve with warm naan bread.

CHICKEN TIKKA

The word tikka *refers to the use of boneless, skinless cubes of chicken breast. Strictly speaking, the term cannot be applied to other types of meat, even if they are prepared and cooked in a similar way. Traditionally cooked in the tandoor (Indian clay oven), chicken tikka is enduringly popular in the West as well as in India.*

SERVES 6

450g/1lb chicken breast fillets, skinned, and cubed
5ml/1 tsp grated fresh root ginger
5ml/1 tsp crushed garlic
5ml/1 tsp chilli powder
1.5ml/¼ tsp ground turmeric
5ml/1 tsp salt
150ml/¼ pint/⅔ cup natural (plain) yogurt
60ml/4 tbsp lemon juice
15ml/1 tbsp chopped fresh coriander (cilantro)
15ml/1 tbsp vegetable oil

To serve (optional)
lettuce
1 small onion, cut into rings
lime wedges
fresh coriander (cilantro)

1 In a large bowl, mix the chicken cubes, ginger, garlic, chilli powder, turmeric, salt, yogurt, lemon juice and coriander. Leave to marinate in a cool place for at least 2 hours, or in the refrigerator overnight.

COOK'S TIP
Thread the meat on to oiled skewers, and turn and baste it during cooking.

2 Place the chicken on a grill (broiler) tray, or in a flameproof dish lined with foil, and baste with the oil.

3 Preheat the grill to medium. Grill (broil) the chicken for 15–20 minutes until cooked, turning and basting two or three times. Serve with lettuce, onion rings, lime wedges and fresh coriander.

SHAMMI KABAB

Kababs came to India from the Middle East, where the word is spelt kebab and refers to a skewered meat. There is a delectable range of kababs in Indian cuisine, most of which can be served either as appetizers or side dishes with an accompanying raita or chutney.

SERVES 5–6

2 onions, finely chopped
250g/9oz lean lamb, boned and cubed
50g/2oz chana dhal or yellow split peas
5ml/1 tsp cumin seeds
5ml/1 tsp garam masala
4–6 fresh green chillies
5cm/2in piece fresh root ginger, grated
175ml/6fl oz/¾ cup water
a few fresh coriander (cilantro) and mint
    leaves, chopped, plus extra coriander
    (cilantro) sprigs to garnish
juice of 1 lemon
15ml/1 tbsp gram flour (besan)
2 eggs, beaten
vegetable oil, for shallow frying
salt

1 Put the first seven ingredients and the water into a large pan with salt, and bring to the boil. Simmer, covered, until the meat and dhal are cooked. Remove the lid and continue to cook for a few more minutes, to reduce the excess liquid. Set aside to cool.

2 Transfer the cooled meat and dhal mixture to a food processor or blender and process to a rough paste.

3 Put the paste into a large mixing bowl and add the chopped coriander and mint leaves, lemon juice and gram flour. Knead well with your hands to make sure the ingredients are evenly distributed through the mixture.

4 Divide the mixture into 10–12 even-size portions and use your hands to roll each into a ball, then flatten slightly. Chill for 1 hour. Dip the kababs in the beaten egg and shallow fry each side until golden brown. Pat dry on kitchen paper and serve hot.

ROGAN JOSH

This is one of the most popular lamb dishes to have originated in Kashmir. Traditionally, fatty meat on the bone is slow cooked until most of the fat is separated from the meat. The fat that escapes from the meat in this way is known as rogan *and* josh *refers to the rich red colour. The Kashmiris achieve this colour by using a combination of mild and bright Kashmiri chillies and the juice extracted from a brightly coloured local flower.*

SERVES 4–6

45ml/3 tbsp lemon juice
250ml/8fl oz/1 cup natural (plain) yogurt
5ml/1 tsp salt
2 garlic cloves, crushed
2.5cm/1in piece fresh root ginger, finely grated
900g/2lb lean lamb fillet, cubed
60ml/4 tbsp vegetable oil
2.5ml/½ tsp cumin seeds
2 bay leaves
4 green cardamom pods
1 onion, finely chopped
10ml/2 tsp ground coriander
10ml/2 tsp ground cumin
5ml/1 tsp chilli powder
400g/14oz can chopped tomatoes
30ml/2 tbsp tomato purée (paste)
150ml/¼ pint/⅔ cup water
toasted cumin seeds and bay leaves, to garnish
plain boiled rice, to serve

1 In a large bowl, mix together the lemon juice, yogurt, salt, one crushed garlic clove and the ginger. Add the lamb and marinate in the refrigerator overnight.

2 Heat the oil in a wok, karahi or large pan and fry the cumin seeds for 2 minutes until they splutter. Add the bay leaves and cardamom pods and fry for 2 minutes.

3 Add the onion and remaining garlic and fry for 5 minutes. Add the coriander, cumin and chilli powder. Fry for 2 minutes.

4 Add the marinated lamb to the pan and cook for a further 5 minutes, stirring occasionally to prevent the mixture from sticking to the base of the pan.

5 Add the tomatoes, tomato purée and water. Cover and simmer for 1–1½ hours. Garnish with toasted cumin seeds and bay leaves, and serve.

MINCED LAMB with PEAS

This dish, known as kheema mattar, *is a favourite all over India, although it originated in the north. Generally, in India minced mutton is used, as lamb is not very easy to obtain. Minced turkey, pork or chicken would all work equally well.*

SERVES 4

45ml/3 tbsp vegetable oil
1 onion, finely chopped
2 garlic cloves, crushed
2.5cm/1in piece fresh root ginger, grated
2 fresh green chillies, finely chopped
675g/1½lb minced (ground) lamb
5ml/1 tsp ground cumin
5ml/1 tsp ground coriander
5ml/1 tsp chilli powder
5ml/1 tsp salt
175g/6oz/1½ cups frozen peas, thawed
30ml/2 tbsp lemon juice
naan and natural (plain) yogurt, to serve

3 Stir in the cumin, coriander, chilli powder and salt with 300ml/½ pint/ 1¼ cups water. Cover the pan and simmer for about 25 minutes.

4 Add the peas and lemon juice. Cook for 10 minutes, uncovered. Garnish with fresh coriander and chilli powder and serve with warm naan and natural yogurt.

1 Heat the oil and fry the onion for about 5 minutes over a medium heat until browned. Add the garlic, ginger and chillies and fry for 2–3 minutes.

2 Add the minced lamb and stir-fry briskly for 5 minutes over a high heat.

COOK'S TIP
To reduce the fat content, dry-fry the lamb in a non-stick frying pan until the natural fat is released. Drain the fat and use the lamb as directed in the recipe.

LAMB with APRICOTS

This recipe comes from the wonderful fruit-laden valley of Kashmir. The cuisine of Kashmir is renowned for the imaginative use of all the exotic fruits and nuts that grow abundantly in that state. Serve with an apricot chutney to complement the fruit in the recipe.

2 Heat the oil in a wok, karahi or large pan and fry the cinnamon stick and cardamoms for 2 minutes. Add the onion and fry for 6–8 minutes until soft.

3 Add the curry paste and fry for about 2 minutes. Stir in the cumin, coriander and salt and fry for 2–3 minutes.

4 Add the cubed lamb, dried apricots and the lamb stock to the pan. Cover with the lid and cook over a medium heat for 1–1½ hours.

SERVES 4–6

900g/2lb stewing lamb
30ml/2 tbsp vegetable oil
2.5cm/1in piece cinnamon stick
4 green cardamom pods
1 onion, chopped
15ml/1 tbsp curry paste
5ml/1 tsp ground cumin
5ml/1 tsp ground coriander
1.5ml/¼ tsp salt
175g/6oz/¾ cup ready-to-eat dried apricots
350ml/12fl oz/1½ cups lamb stock
fresh coriander (cilantro), to garnish

1 Cut away and discard any visible fat from the lamb, then cut the meat into 2.5cm/1in cubes.

5 Transfer to a serving dish and garnish with the fresh coriander. Classic Pulao and Apricot Chutney would make good accompaniments to this dish.

LAMB KOFTA CURRY

Koftas, or meatballs, reveal a Middle Eastern influence on Indian cuisine. The Middle Eastern technique for making the meatballs is still used, combined with the skilful blending of Indian spices. Koftas make an inexpensive but delicious main course.

SERVES 4

675g/1½lb minced (ground) lamb
1 fresh green chilli, roughly chopped
1 garlic clove, chopped
2.5cm/1in piece fresh root ginger, chopped
1.5ml/¼ tsp garam masala
1.5ml/¼ tsp salt
45ml/3 tbsp chopped fresh coriander
   (cilantro)

For the sauce
30ml/2 tbsp vegetable oil
2.5ml/½ tsp cumin seeds
1 onion, chopped
1 garlic clove, chopped
2.5cm/1in piece fresh root ginger,
   grated
5ml/1 tsp ground cumin
5ml/1 tsp ground coriander
2.5ml/½ tsp salt
2.5ml/½ tsp chilli powder
15ml/1 tbsp tomato purée (paste)
400g/14oz can chopped tomatoes
fresh coriander (cilantro) sprigs,
   to garnish
coriander (cilantro) rice, to serve

1 To make the meatballs, put the lamb, chilli, garlic, ginger, garam masala, salt and coriander into a food processor and process until the mixture binds together.

2 Shape the mixture into 16 balls, using your hands. Cover with clear film (plastic wrap) and chill for 10 minutes.

COOK'S TIP
You can make the meatballs the day before. Store them in the refrigerator until needed.

3 To make the sauce, heat the oil and fry the cumin seeds until they splutter. Add the onion, garlic and ginger and fry for 5 minutes. Stir in the remaining sauce ingredients and simmer for 5 minutes.

4 Add the meatballs. Bring to the boil, cover and simmer for 25–30 minutes, or until the meatballs are cooked through. Garnish with sprigs of fresh coriander and serve with coriander rice.

KARAHI POTATOES with WHOLE SPICES

*All spices work like magic with potatoes. Even just a light touch can bring about a
complete transformation. For this recipe choose floury potatoes, as they will absorb
the spice flavours better than the waxy variety.*

SERVES 4

45ml/3 tbsp vegetable oil
2.5ml/½ tsp white cumin seeds
3 curry leaves
5ml/1 tsp crushed dried red chillies
2.5ml/½ tsp mixed onion, mustard
   and fenugreek seeds
2.5ml/½ tsp fennel seeds
3 garlic cloves, roughly chopped
2.5ml/½ tsp grated fresh root ginger
2 onions, sliced
6 new potatoes, cut into 5mm/¼in slices
15ml/1 tbsp chopped fresh coriander
   (cilantro)
1 fresh red chilli, seeded and sliced
1 fresh green chilli, seeded and sliced

1 Heat the oil in a wok, karahi or large
pan. Lower the heat slightly and add the
cumin seeds, curry leaves, dried chillies,
mixed onion, mustard and fenugreek
seeds, fennel seeds, chopped garlic and
grated ginger.

2 Fry for about 1 minute, then add the
sliced onions and fry gently for a further
5 minutes, or until the onions are golden
brown. Add the sliced potatoes, fresh
coriander and red and green chillies. Mix
together well. Cover the pan tightly with
a lid or foil, making sure the foil does
not touch the food. Cook over a very
low heat for about 7 minutes, or until
the potatoes are tender.

3 Remove the lid or foil from the
pan and serve the potatoes hot with
parathas and any lentil dish for a
vegetarian meal. Serve Shammi Kabab,
Tandoori Chicken or Chicken Tikka
instead of the lentils for meat eaters.

MUSHROOM CURRY

In India, mushrooms traditionally grow only in the northern state of Kashmir. However, Indians have acquired the taste for them due to frequent travels abroad, and they are now being cultivated in other northern areas where the climate is suitable.

2 Add the onion and fry for 5 minutes or until golden. Stir in the ground cumin, coriander and garam masala and fry for a further 2 minutes.

3 Add the chilli, garlic and ginger and fry for 2–3 minutes, stirring constantly. Add the tomatoes and salt. Bring to the boil and simmer for 5 minutes.

SERVES 4

30ml/2 tbsp vegetable oil
2.5ml/½ tsp cumin seeds
1.5ml/¼ tsp black peppercorns
4 green cardamom pods
1.5ml/¼ tsp ground turmeric
1 onion, finely chopped
5ml/1 tsp ground cumin
5ml/1 tsp ground coriander
2.5ml/½ tsp garam masala
1 fresh green chilli, finely chopped
2 garlic cloves, crushed
2.5cm/1in piece fresh root ginger, grated
400g/4oz can chopped tomatoes
1.5ml/¼ tsp salt
450g/1lb/6 cups button (white) mushrooms
chopped fresh coriander (cilantro),
   to garnish

1 Heat the vegetable oil in a wok, karahi or large pan and fry the cumin seeds, black peppercorns, cardamom pods and turmeric for 2–3 minutes.

COOK'S TIP
For authentic Kashmiri style, use ground or crushed fennel in place of the cumin.

4 Halve the mushrooms, then add them to the pan. Cover and simmer over a low heat for 10 minutes. Transfer to a warm serving platter and garnish with chopped coriander. Serve with an Indian bread, such as naan, parathas or chapatis, and any dry meat or poultry dish, such as Shammi Kabab or Tandoori Chicken.

COURGETTES in SPICED TOMATO SAUCE

In India, tender marrow would be used for this recipe as courgettes are not grown there. Do try this recipe with a young marrow in the summer. It will also work well with winter squashes, such as butternut and acorn.

SERVES 4

675g/1½lb courgettes (zucchini)
45ml/3 tbsp vegetable oil
2.5ml/½ tsp cumin seeds
2.5ml/½ tsp mustard seeds
1 onion, thinly sliced
2 garlic cloves, crushed
1.5ml/¼ tsp ground turmeric
1.5ml/¼ tsp chilli powder
5ml/1 tsp ground coriander
5ml/1 tsp ground cumin
2.5ml/½ tsp salt
15ml/1 tbsp tomato purée (paste)
400g/14oz can chopped tomatoes
150ml/¼ pint/⅔ cup water
15ml/1 tbsp chopped fresh coriander
    (cilantro)
5ml/1 tsp garam masala

1 Trim the ends from the courgettes then cut them into 1cm/½in thick slices.

2 Heat the oil in a wok, karahi or large pan. Fry the cumin and mustard seeds for 2 minutes until they begin to splutter.

3 Add the onion and garlic and fry for about 5–6 minutes.

4 Add the ground turmeric, chilli powder, coriander, cumin and salt and fry for about 2–3 minutes.

5 Add the sliced courgettes, and cook for 5 minutes. Add the tomato purée and chopped tomatoes to the pan.

6 Add the water, then cover the pan and simmer for 10 minutes until the sauce thickens. Stir in the fresh coriander and garam masala, then cook for about 5 minutes, or until the courgettes are tender. Serve as an accompaniment to any meat, poultry or fish dish.

CUMIN-SCENTED VEGETABLES with TOASTED ALMONDS

Cabbage is a traditional vegetable in India, although neither baby corn cobs nor mangetouts are used in Indian cooking. Nonetheless, combining new and traditional ideas can create exciting and original dishes, as this recipe shows.

SERVES 4

15ml/1 tbsp vegetable oil
50g/2oz/4 tbsp butter
2.5ml/½ tsp crushed coriander seeds
2.5ml/½ tsp white cumin seeds
6 dried red chillies
1 small savoy cabbage, shredded
12 mangetouts (snow peas)
3 fresh red chillies, seeded and sliced
12 baby corn cobs, halved
salt
25g/1oz/¼ cup flaked (sliced) almonds, toasted and 15ml/1 tbsp chopped fresh coriander (cilantro), to garnish

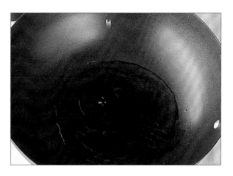

1 Heat the oil and butter in a wok, karahi or large pan and add the crushed coriander seeds, white cumin seeds and dried red chillies.

2 Add the shredded cabbage and mangetouts to the spices in the pan and stir-fry briskly for about 5 minutes, until the cabbage starts to turn crisp.

3 Add the fresh red chillies, and baby corn cobs to the pan and season with salt to taste. Stir-fry for 3 minutes more.

4 Garnish with the toasted almonds and fresh coriander, and serve hot. This dish would go well with any meat curry and with Classic Pulao.

COOK'S TIP
Julienne strips of other vegetables will make this dish visually more appealing, and will add superb taste at the same time. Try julienne carrots and leeks instead of mangetouts and baby corn. Add the cabbage and carrots together, and add the leeks in step 3.

ROASTED AUBERGINES with SPRING ONIONS

This classic dish, made of roasted and mashed aubergines cooked with spring onions, is known as bharta *in the Punjab region. The term* bharta *means to mash. Traditionally, the aubergine is roasted over charcoal, but a hot electric or gas oven will produce similar results, although the smoky flavour will be missing.*

SERVES 4

2 large aubergines (eggplant)
45ml/3 tbsp vegetable oil
2.5ml/½ tsp black mustard seeds
1 bunch spring onions (scallions),
    finely chopped
115g/4oz/1½ cups button (white)
    mushrooms, halved
2 garlic cloves, crushed
1 fresh red chilli, finely chopped
2.5ml/½ tsp chilli powder
5ml/1 tsp ground cumin
5ml/1 tsp ground coriander
1.5ml/¼ tsp ground turmeric
5ml/1 tsp salt
400g/14oz can chopped tomatoes
15ml/1 tbsp chopped fresh coriander
    (cilantro), plus a few extra sprigs
    to garnish

1 Preheat the oven to 200°C/400°F/ Gas 6. Brush both of the aubergines with 15ml/1 tbsp of oil and prick with a fork. Bake for 30–35 minutes until soft.

2 Meanwhile, heat the remaining oil and fry the black mustard seeds for about 2 minutes until they splutter. Add the onions, mushrooms, garlic and chilli, and fry for 5 minutes more. Stir in the chilli powder, cumin, coriander, turmeric and salt and fry for 3–4 minutes. Add the tomatoes and simmer for 5 minutes.

COOK'S TIP
Roast the aubergines (eggplant) over a barbecue for an authentic smoky flavour.

3 Cut the aubergines in half lengthwise and scoop out the soft flesh into a large mixing bowl. Mash the flesh to a course texture, using a fork.

4 Add the aubergines to the pan with the coriander. Bring to the boil and simmer for 5 minutes until the sauce thickens. Serve garnished with coriander.

KIDNEY BEAN CURRY

This dish, known as rajma *in Punjabi, is a fine example of the area's hearty, robust cuisine. It is widely eaten dish all over the state, and is even sold by street vendors. Plain boiled rice makes the perfect accompaniment for this dish.*

2 Drain the beans and place in a large pan with double the volume of water. Boil vigorously for 10 minutes. Drain, rinse and return the beans to the pan. Add double the volume of water and bring to the boil. Reduce the heat, then cover and cook for 1–1½ hours, or until the beans are soft. This process is essential in order to remove the toxins that are present in dried kidney beans.

3 Meanwhile, heat the oil in a wok, karahi or large pan and fry the cumin seeds for 2 minutes until they begin to splutter. Add the onion, chilli, garlic and ginger and fry for 5 minutes. Stir in the curry paste, cumin, coriander, chilli powder and salt, and cook for 5 minutes.

4 Add the tomatoes and simmer for 5 minutes. Add the beans and fresh coriander, reserving a little for the garnish. Cover and cook for 15 minutes adding a little water if necessary. Serve garnished with the reserved coriander.

SERVES 4

225g/8oz/1¼ cups dried red kidney beans
30ml/2 tbsp vegetable oil
2.5ml/½ tsp cumin seeds
1 onion, thinly sliced
1 fresh green chilli, finely chopped
2 garlic cloves, crushed
2.5cm/1in piece fresh root ginger, grated
30ml/2 tbsp curry paste
5ml/1 tsp ground cumin
5ml/1 tsp ground coriander
2.5ml/½ tsp chilli powder
2.5ml/½ tsp salt
400g/14oz can chopped tomatoes
30ml/2 tbsp chopped fresh
    coriander (cilantro)

1 Place the kidney beans in a large bowl of cold water and then leave them to soak overnight.

COOK'S TIP
Drained and well-rinsed canned beans work very well as an alternative.

CREAMY BLACK LENTILS

Black lentils or urad dhal *are available whole, split, and skinned and split. Generally, both split, and skinned and split versions are used in west and south Indian cooking, whereas whole black lentils are a typical ingredient in the north.*

SERVES 4–6

175g/6oz/¾ cup black lentils, soaked
50g/2oz/¼ cup red split lentils
120ml/4fl oz/½ cup double (heavy) cream
120ml/4fl oz/½ cup natural (plain) yogurt
5ml/1 tsp cornflour (cornstarch)
45ml/3 tbsp ghee or vegetable oil
1 onion, finely chopped
5cm/2in piece fresh root ginger, crushed
4 fresh green chillies, chopped
1 tomato, chopped
2.5ml/½ tsp chilli powder
2.5ml/½ tsp ground turmeric
2.5ml/½ tsp ground cumin
2 garlic cloves, sliced
salt
coriander (cilantro) sprigs and sliced
    red chilli, to garnish

3 Heat 15ml/1 tbsp of the ghee or oil in a wok, karahi or large pan, and fry the onion, ginger, two green chillies and the tomato until the onion is soft. Add the ground spices and salt and fry for a further 2 minutes. Stir into the lentil mixture and mix well. Reheat, transfer to a heatproof serving dish and keep warm.

4 Heat the remaining ghee or oil in a frying pan over a low heat and fry the garlic slices and remaining chillies until the garlic slices are golden brown. Pour over the lentils and fold the garlic and chilli into the lentils just before serving. Place extra cream on the table for the diners to add more if they wish.

1 Drain the black lentils and place in a large pan with the red lentils. Cover with water and bring to the boil. Reduce the heat, cover the pan and simmer until tender. Mash with a spoon, and cool.

2 In a bowl, mix together the cream, yogurt and cornflour, and stir into the lentils in the pan.

EAST INDIA

The state of Bengal has developed a strong culinary identity, which makes use of local produce such as mustard, coconut, vegetables, lentils and rice. Fish from the Bay of Bengal is eaten throughout eastern India, and in areas close to the sea, fish is eaten daily, in place of meat.

CHICKEN JHALFRAZI

Jhalfrazi was created by Indian chefs during the British Raj. Leftover cold meat, generally from the Sunday roast, was stir-fried with spices. The dish originated in Calcutta, where the East India Company was established as an important trading post by the British.

SERVES 4

675g/1½lb chicken breast fillets, skinned
30ml/2 tbsp vegetable oil
5ml/1 tsp cumin seeds
1 onion, finely chopped
1 green (bell) pepper, finely chopped
1 red (bell) pepper, finely chopped
1 garlic clove, crushed
2cm/¾in piece fresh root ginger, chopped
15ml/1 tbsp curry paste
1.5ml/¼ tsp chilli powder
5ml/1 tsp ground coriander
5ml/1 tsp ground cumin
2.5ml/½ tsp salt
400g/14oz can chopped tomatoes
30ml/2 tbsp chopped fresh coriander
   (cilantro)
fresh coriander (cilantro) sprig, to garnish
plain boiled rice or naan bread, to serve

3 Add the curry paste to the other ingredients in the pan and stir-fry for about 2 minutes. Stir in the chilli powder, ground coriander, cumin and salt, and add 15ml/1 tbsp water. Stir-fry for a further 2 minutes.

4 Add the chicken and stir-fry for about 5 minutes. Add the tomatoes and fresh coriander. Cook, covered, for about 15 minutes until the chicken is tender. Garnish with a sprig of fresh coriander. Serve with plain boiled rice or naan.

1 Remove any visible fat and cut the chicken into 2.5cm/1in cubes.

2 Heat the oil in a wok, karahi or large pan, and fry the cumin seeds for 30–40 seconds until they begin to splutter. Add the onion, peppers, garlic and ginger and fry for 6–8 minutes.

MASALA CHANNA

This is a typical Calcutta street food known as ghughni. *Plates full of* ghughni, *with the wholesome taste of chickpeas laced with spices and tamarind juice, are enjoyed with flat breads such as chapatis and parathas.*

SERVES 4

225g/8oz/1¼ cups dried chickpeas
50g/2oz tamarind pulp
120ml/4fl oz/½ cup boiling water
45ml/3 tbsp vegetable oil
2.5ml/½ tsp cumin seeds
1 onion, finely chopped
2 garlic cloves, crushed
2.5cm/1in piece fresh root ginger, grated
1 fresh green chilli, finely chopped
5ml/1 tsp ground cumin
5ml/1 tsp ground coriander
1.5ml/¼ tsp ground turmeric
2.5ml/½ tsp salt
225g/8oz tomatoes, skinned and
    finely chopped
2.5ml/½ tsp garam masala
chopped chillies and chopped onion,
    to garnish

1 Put the chickpeas in a large bowl and cover with plenty of cold water. Leave to soak overnight.

2 Drain the chickpeas and place in a large pan with double the volume of cold water. Bring to the boil and boil vigorously for 10 minutes. Skim off any scum, then cover and simmer for 1½–2 hours or until soft.

3 Meanwhile, break up the tamarind pulp and soak in the boiling water for about 15 minutes. Use the back of a spoon to rub the tamarind through a sieve (strainer) into a bowl, discarding any stones and fibre. (Leave out this step if you are using commercial tamarind paste in place of the fresh pulp.)

4 Heat the vegetable oil in a wok, karahi or large pan and fry the cumin seeds for 2 minutes until they begin to splutter. Add the chopped onion, garlic, ginger and chilli and fry for 5 minutes.

5 Add the cumin, coriander, turmeric and salt and fry for 3–4 minutes. Add the tomatoes and tamarind juice. Bring to the boil and simmer for 5 minutes.

6 Add the chickpeas and garam masala, cover and simmer for about 15 minutes. Garnish with the chillies and onion.

COOK'S TIP
Make double the quantity of tamarind juice and freeze in ice-cube trays. It will keep for up to 12 months. Alternatively, buy tamarind paste sold in Indian stores. It is ready to use and will keep for an indefinite period at room temperature.

SOUTH INDIA

The food in the southern states is light and refreshing, with plenty of
fish and shellfish; it is also fiery, with much use being made of the
chillies that are grown throughout the region. In south India, coconut
milk is used to enrich sauces in place of the dairy cream and nuts
used in the north.

MUGHLAI-STYLE CHICKEN

The cuisine of Andhra Pradesh is renowned for its pungency because the hottest variety of chilli is grown there. In sharp contrast, however, the region is also home to the subtle flavours of a style of cooking known as nizami, which has a distinct Mogul influence. This recipe, with the heady aroma of saffron and the captivating flavour of a silky almond and cream sauce, is a typical example.

SERVES 4–6

4 chicken breast fillets, rubbed with
   a little garam masala
2 eggs, beaten with salt and pepper
90ml/6 tbsp ghee or vegetable oil
1 large onion, finely chopped
5cm/2in piece fresh root ginger,
   finely crushed
4 garlic cloves, finely crushed
4 cloves
4 green cardamom pods
5cm/2in piece cinnamon stick
2 bay leaves
15–20 saffron threads
150ml/¼ pint/⅔ cup natural (plain)
   yogurt, beaten with 5ml/1 tsp
   cornflour (cornstarch)
75ml/5 tbsp/⅓ cup double (heavy) cream
50g/2oz ground almonds
salt

3 Return the chicken to the pan, along with any juices, and gently cook until the chicken is tender. Adjust the seasoning if necessary.

4 Just before serving, fold in the double cream and ground almonds. Make sure the curry is piping hot before serving. Tricolour Pulao goes well with this dish.

1 Brush the chicken fillets with the beaten eggs. In a wok, karahi or large pan, heat the ghee or vegetable oil and fry the chicken until cooked through and browned on both sides. Remove the chicken from the pan and keep warm.

2 In the same pan, fry the chopped onion, ginger, garlic, cloves, cardamom pods, cinnamon and bay leaves. When the onion turns golden, remove the pan from the heat, allow the contents to cool a little and add the saffron and natural yogurt. Mix well to prevent the yogurt from curdling.

CHICKEN MADRAS

Madras, one of India's largest cities, is the capital of Tamil Nadu. The city is generally regarded as the heartland of southern Indian cuisine. It is surrounded by long stretches of beautiful beaches, shared between the Bay of Bengal to the east and the Indian Ocean to the south. The food is mainly vegetarian, but the small Muslim and Christian communities have a wonderful range of meat- and poultry-based dishes, such as this one.

SERVES 4

450g/1lb chicken breast fillets, skinned
45ml/3 tbsp tomato purée (paste)
large pinch ground fenugreek
1.5ml/¼ tsp ground fennel seeds
5ml/1 tsp grated fresh root ginger
7.5ml/1½ tsp ground coriander
5ml/1 tsp crushed garlic
5ml/1 tsp chilli powder
1.5ml/¼ tsp ground turmeric
30ml/2 tbsp lemon juice
5ml/1 tsp salt
300ml/½ pint/1¼ cups water
45ml/3 tbsp vegetable oil
2 onions, diced
2–4 curry leaves
2 fresh green chillies, seeded
  and chopped
15ml/1 tbsp chopped fresh coriander
  (cilantro), plus extra sprigs to garnish
naan bread, to serve

1 Cut the chicken breast fillets into cubes. Mix the tomato purée in a bowl with the fenugreek, fennel, ginger, ground coriander, garlic, chilli powder, turmeric, lemon juice, salt and water.

2 Heat the oil in a wok, karahi or large pan and fry the onions with the curry leaves until the onions are golden. Add the chicken and stir for 1 minute to seal.

COOK'S TIP
Take care not to use too much ground fenugreek, as it can be quite bitter.

3 Pour the tomato sauce and spice mixture into the pan. Stir for 2 minutes to ensure the ingredients are well mixed.

4 Lower the heat and cook for 8–10 minutes, then add the chillies and fresh coriander. Garnish and serve.

BEEF with GREEN BEANS

Adding vegetables to meat and poultry dishes has been a long-standing practice in Indian cooking. As well as resulting in some interesting combinations, the technique is a practical one, as the final dish makes a nutritious one-pot meal. Although red pepper is not normally used, it does provide visual appeal as well as enhanced flavour. As an alternative, you could use fresh red chillies. Leaving the chillies whole will provide a wonderful flavour without the pungency, but if you like it hot, slit them first to expose the seeds.

SERVES 4

275g/10oz fine green beans, cut into
   2.5cm/1in pieces
45–60ml/3–4 tbsp vegetable oil
1 onion, sliced
5ml/1 tsp grated fresh root ginger
5ml/1 tsp crushed garlic
5ml/1 tsp chilli powder
6.5ml/1¼ tsp ground turmeric
2 tomatoes, chopped
450g/1lb beef, cubed
475ml/16fl oz/2 cups water
1 red (bell) pepper, sliced (optional)
15ml/1 tbsp chopped fresh coriander
   (cilantro)
2 fresh green chillies, chopped
salt

3 Mix together the ginger, crushed garlic, chilli powder, salt, turmeric and chopped tomatoes. Spoon this mixture into the onions in the pan and stir-fry for 5–7 minutes.

4 Add the beef and stir-fry for a further 3 minutes. Pour in the water, bring to the boil and then lower the heat. Half cover the pan and cook for 1–1¼ hours, until most of the water has evaporated and the meat is tender.

5 Add the green beans to the pan and mix everything together well.

1 Boil the green beans in salted water for about 3 minutes, then drain and set them aside.

2 Heat the oil in a large pan over a medium heat and fry the sliced onion until it turns golden brown (this should take about 7–8 minutes).

COOK'S TIP
You could use lamb or turkey thigh meat instead of beef. If using turkey, reduce the quantity of water by half.

6 Finally, add the red pepper, if using, with the chopped fresh coriander and green chillies and cook, stirring, for a further 7–10 minutes. Serve the curry hot. This dish would go very well with Nut Pulao.

MADRAS BEEF CURRY

Although Madras is renowned for the best vegetarian food in the country, meat-based recipes such as this one are also extremely popular. This particular recipe is a contribution by the area's small Muslim community.

SERVES 4–6

60ml/4 tbsp vegetable oil
1 large onion, finely sliced
3–4 cloves
4 green cardamoms
2 whole star anise
4 fresh green chillies, chopped
2 fresh or dried red chillies, chopped
45ml/3 tbsp Madras masala paste
5ml/1 tsp ground turmeric
450g/1lb lean beef, cubed
60ml/4 tbsp tamarind juice
granulated sugar, to taste
salt
a few fresh coriander (cilantro) leaves,
    chopped, to garnish

1 Heat the vegetable oil in a wok, karahi or large pan over a medium heat and fry the onion slices for 8–9 minutes until they turn golden brown. Lower the heat, add all the spice ingredients, and fry for a further 2–3 minutes.

2 Add the beef and mix well. Cover and cook on low heat until the beef is tender. Cook uncovered on a higher heat for the last few minutes to reduce any excess liquid.

COOK'S TIP
To tenderize the meat, add 60ml/4 tbsp white wine vinegar in step 2, along with the meat, and omit the tamarind juice.

3 Fold in the tamarind juice, sugar and salt. Reheat the dish and garnish with the chopped coriander leaves. Tricolour Pulao and Tomato and Onion Salad would both make excellent accompaniments to this dish.

LENTILS SEASONED with GARLIC-INFUSED OIL

This recipe, known as sambhar, varies considerably within the southern states. Vegetables
are added to the lentils, and this can be a single vegetable or a combination of two or
more. It is traditionally served with steamed rice dumplings (idlis) or stuffed rice pancakes
(dosai). It is also extremely satisfying with plain boiled rice.

SERVES 4–6

120ml/8 tbsp vegetable oil
2.5ml/½ tsp mustard seeds
2.5ml/½ tsp cumin seeds
2 dried red chillies
1.5ml/¼ tsp asafoetida
6–8 curry leaves
2 garlic cloves, crushed, plus 2 garlic
    cloves, sliced
30ml/2 tbsp desiccated (dry, unsweetened,
    shredded) coconut
225g/8oz/1 cup red lentils, picked over,
    washed and drained
10ml/2 tsp sambhar masala
2.5ml/½ tsp ground turmeric
450ml/¾ pint/scant 2 cups water
450g/1lb mixed vegetables, such as okra,
    courgettes (zucchini), aubergine
    (eggplant) cauliflower, shallots and
    (bell) peppers
60ml/4 tbsp tamarind juice
4 firm tomatoes, quartered
a few coriander (cilantro) leaves, chopped

2 Cover the pan and leave to simmer
for 25–30 minutes, until the lentils are
mushy. Add the mixed vegetables,
tamarind juice and tomato quarters.
Cook until the vegetables are just tender.

3 Heat the remaining oil in a small pan
over a low heat, and fry the garlic slices
until golden. Stir in the coriander leaves,
then pour over the lentils and vegetables.
Mix at the table before serving.

1 Heat half the oil in a wok, karahi or
large pan, and stir-fry the next seven
ingredients until the coconut begins to
brown. Stir in the prepared red lentils,
sambhar masala and turmeric. Stir-fry for
2–3 minutes and add the water. Bring it
to the boil and reduce the heat to low.

COOK'S TIP
Red lentils are used in this recipe, but the
traditional choice would be yellow split
lentils, known as toor dhal or tuvar dhal,
which are available from Indian stores.

STUFFED BANANAS

Bananas are cooked with spices in many different ways in southern India. Some recipes contain large quantities of chillies, but the taste is skilfully mellowed by adding coconut milk and tamarind juice. Green bananas are available from Indian stores, or you can use plantains or unripe eating bananas that are firm to the touch.

SERVES 4

4 green bananas or plantains
30ml/2 tbsp ground coriander
15ml/1 tbsp ground cumin
5ml/1 tsp chilli powder
2.5ml/½ tsp salt
1.5ml/¼ tsp ground turmeric
5ml/1 tsp granulated sugar
15ml/1 tbsp gram flour (besan)
45ml/3 tbsp chopped fresh coriander
    (cilantro), plus extra sprigs
    to garnish
90ml/6 tbsp vegetable oil
1.5ml/¼ tsp cumin seeds
1.5ml/¼ tsp black mustard seeds

1 Trim the bananas or plantains and cut each crossways into three equal pieces, leaving the skin on. Make a lengthwise slit along each piece of banana, without cutting all the way through the flesh.

2 On a plate mix together the ground coriander, cumin, chilli powder, salt, turmeric, sugar, gram flour, chopped fresh coriander and 15ml/1 tbsp of the oil. Use your fingers to combine well.

3 Carefully stuff each piece of banana with the spice mixture, taking care not to break the bananas in half.

4 Heat the remaining oil in a wok, karahi or large pan, and fry the cumin and mustard seeds for 2 minutes or until they begin to splutter. Add the bananas and toss gently in the oil. Cover and simmer over a low heat for 15 minutes, stirring from time to time, until the bananas are soft but not mushy.

5 Garnish with the fresh coriander sprigs, and serve with warm chapatis, if you like. Other good accompaniments include Prawn Biryani and Spiced Yogurt.

COOK'S TIP
Baby courgettes (zucchini) would make a delicious alternative to bananas.

SPICED LENTILS with SPINACH

Spinach cooked with chana dhal lentils makes a wholesome, healthy dish. It is perfect for a vegetarian diet, as it provides protein, vitamins and minerals in one dish. Serve it with naan bread, chapatis or plain boiled rice to make a satisfying main course. A salad or a chutney will add an extra special zest to the meal.

2 Drain the chana dhal or split peas and put in a large pan with the water. Bring to the boil, cover, and simmer for about 20–25 minutes until the dhal are soft. Cook, uncovered, until the cooking liquid has evaporated completely.

3 Heat the oil in a wok, karahi or large pan and fry the mustard seeds for about 2 minutes until they begin to splutter. Add the onion, garlic, ginger and chilli and fry for 5–6 minutes, then add the spinach and cook for 10 minutes or until the spinach is dry and the liquid is absorbed. Stir in the remaining spices and salt and cook for 2–3 minutes.

4 Add the chana dhal or split peas to the spinach in the pan and cook, stirring, for about 5 minutes. Serve hot with warm naan bread, or with plain boiled rice, if you like.

SERVES 4

175g/6oz/¾ cup chana dhal or yellow
   split peas
175ml/6fl oz/¾ cup water
30ml/2 tbsp vegetable oil
1.5ml/¼ tsp black mustard seeds
1 onion, thinly sliced
2 garlic cloves, crushed
2.5cm/1in piece fresh root ginger, grated
1 red chilli, finely chopped
275g/10oz frozen spinach, thawed
1.5ml/¼ tsp chilli powder
2.5ml/½ tsp ground coriander
2.5ml/½ tsp garam masala
2.5ml/½ tsp salt

1 Wash the chana dhal or split peas in several changes of cold water. Put the dhal or peas into a large bowl and cover with plenty of cold water. Leave to soak for about 30 minutes.

COOK'S TIP
Use canned chickpeas in place of chana dhal for a quick alternative. Drain, rinse in water, drain again, and add in step 4.

WEST INDIA

The western states of Gujarat and Maharashtra have developed an excellent repertoire of vegetarian dishes, using fresh vegetables, dairy products and lentils and peas. Goa, to the south of Bombay, shows Portuguese influences; its most famous culinary export is vindaloo.

GOAN PRAWN CURRY

The cuisine of Goa is well known for its excellent range of fish and shellfish-based recipes, such as this one for prawns. Numerous varieties of fish and shellfish are found along the extended coastline and the network of inland waterways.

SERVES 4

15g/½oz/1 tbsp ghee or butter
2 garlic cloves, crushed
450g/1lb small raw prawns (shrimp), peeled and deveined
15ml/1 tbsp groundnut (peanut) oil
4 cardamom pods
4 cloves
5cm/2in piece cinnamon stick
15ml/1 tbsp mustard seeds
1 large onion, finely chopped
½–1 fresh red chilli, seeded and sliced
4 tomatoes, peeled, seeded and chopped
175ml/6fl oz/¾ cup fish stock or water
350ml/12fl oz/1½ cups coconut milk
45ml/3 tbsp Fragrant Spice Mix (see Cook's Tip)
10–20ml/2–4 tsp chilli powder
salt
turmeric-coloured basmati rice, to serve

1 Melt the ghee or butter in a wok, karahi or large pan, add the garlic and stir over a low heat for a few seconds. Add the prawns and stir-fry briskly to coat. Transfer to a plate and set aside.

VARIATION
For a reduced fat version, use the same quantity of semi-skimmed (low-fat) milk instead of the coconut milk.

2 In the same pan, heat the oil and fry the cardamom, cloves and cinnamon for 2 minutes. Add the mustard seeds and fry for 1 minute. Add the onion and chilli and fry for 7–8 minutes or until softened and lightly browned.

3 Add the remaining ingredients and bring to a slow simmer. Cook gently for 6–8 minutes and add the prawns. Simmer for 5–8 minutes until the prawns are cooked through. Serve the curry with turmeric-coloured basmati rice.

COOK'S TIP
To make a Fragrant Spice Mix, dry-fry 25ml/1½ tbsp coriander seeds, 15ml/1 tbsp mixed peppercorns, 5ml/1 tsp cumin seeds, 1.5ml/¼ tsp fenugreek seeds and 1.5ml/¼ tsp fennel seeds until aromatic, then grind finely in a spice mill.

PARSI PRAWN CURRY

After landing on the west coast of India, the Parsi community migrated to different parts of the country. The majority, however, made Bombay their home. They have cleverly integrated their cooking style into the exotic tastes of Indian cuisine, as this curry shows.

2 Add the chopped onions to the other ingredients in the pan and fry gently until the chopped onions become translucent, then fold in the tamarind juice, mint sauce, sugar and salt. Simmer for a further 3 minutes.

3 Carefully peel and devein the king prawns, then pat them dry with kitchen paper. Add the prawns to the spice mixture with a small amount of water and stir-fry until the prawns turn bright orange/pink.

SERVES 4–6

60ml/4 tbsp vegetable oil
1 onion, finely sliced, plus 2 onions,
   finely chopped
6 garlic cloves, crushed
5ml/1 tsp chilli powder
7.5ml/1½ tsp ground turmeric
50ml/2fl oz/¼ cup tamarind juice
5ml/1 tsp mint sauce
15ml/1 tbsp demerara (raw) sugar
450g/1lb raw king prawns (jumbo shrimp)
75g/3oz coriander (cilantro) leaves,
   chopped, plus extra leaves to garnish
salt

1 Heat the oil and fry the sliced onion. In a bowl, mix the garlic, chilli powder and turmeric with water to form a paste. Add to the onion and cook.

4 When the prawns are cooked, add the coriander leaves and stir-fry on a high heat to thicken the sauce. Garnish with extra coriander leaves and serve.

FISH CAKES

Goan fish and shellfish are skilfully prepared with spices to make cakes of all shapes and sizes, while the rest of India makes fish kababs. Although haddock is used in this recipe, you can use other less expensive white fish, such as coley or whiting.

MAKES 20

450g/1lb skinned haddock or cod
2 potatoes, peeled, boiled and
    coarsely mashed
4 spring onions (scallions),
    finely chopped
4 fresh green chillies, finely chopped
5cm/2in piece fresh root ginger, crushed
a few coriander (cilantro) and mint
    sprigs, chopped
2 eggs
breadcrumbs, for coating
vegetable oil, for shallow frying
salt and ground black pepper
lemon wedges and chilli sauce,
    to serve

1 Place the skinned fish in a lightly greased steamer and steam gently until cooked. Remove the steamer from the hob (stovetop) but leave the fish on the steaming tray until cool.

2 When the fish is cool, crumble it coarsely into a large bowl, using a fork. Mix in the mashed potatoes, spring onions, chillies, crushed ginger, chopped coriander and mint, and one of the eggs. Season to taste with salt and pepper.

COOK'S TIP
For a quick version, used canned tuna in brine and omit step 1. Make sure the tuna is thoroughly drained before use.

3 Shape into cakes. Beat the remaining egg and dip the cakes in it, then coat with the breadcrumbs. Heat the oil and fry the cakes until brown on all sides. Serve as an appetizer or as a side dish, with the lemon wedges and chilli sauce.

SPICY OMELETTE

Another popular contribution by the Parsis, this irresistible omelette is known as poro in their language. Parsi food originated along the shores of the Caspian Sea, and the cuisine offers some unique flavours, which appeal to both Eastern and Western palates.

SERVES 4–6

30ml/2 tbsp vegetable oil
1 onion, finely chopped
2.5ml/½ tsp ground cumin
1 garlic clove, crushed
1 or 2 fresh green chillies, finely chopped
a few coriander (cilantro) sprigs,
    chopped, plus extra, to garnish
1 firm tomato, chopped
1 small potato, cubed and boiled
25g/1oz/¼ cup cooked peas
25g/1oz/¼ cup cooked sweetcorn,
    or canned sweetcorn, drained
2 eggs, beaten
25g/1oz/¼ cup grated cheese
salt and ground black pepper

1 Heat the vegetable oil in a wok, karahi or large pan, and fry the next nine ingredients until they are well blended but the potato and tomato are still firm. Season to taste with salt and ground black pepper.

2 Increase the heat and pour in the beaten eggs. Reduce the heat, cover and cook until the bottom layer is brown. Turn the omelette over and sprinkle with the grated cheese. Place under a hot grill (broiler) and cook until the egg sets and the cheese has melted.

3 Garnish the omelette with sprigs of coriander and serve with salad for a light lunch. If you prefer, serve it for breakfast, in the typical Parsi style.

VARIATION
You can use any vegetable with the potatoes. Try thickly sliced button (white) mushrooms, added in step 1.

EGGS BAKED on CHIPSTICKS

This is an unusual and delicious way of combining eggs with potato sticks, and is known as sali pur eeda *in the Parsi language. The potato sticks are cooked with spices to form a pancake. Eggs are then placed on top of the potato pancake and gently cooked.*

SERVES 4–6

225g/8oz salted chipsticks
2 fresh green chillies, finely chopped
a few coriander (cilantro) sprigs, chopped
1.5ml/¼ tsp ground turmeric
60ml/4 tbsp vegetable oil
75ml/5 tbsp water
6 eggs
3 spring onions (scallions), finely chopped
salt and ground black pepper

1 In a bowl, mix the salted chipsticks, chopped chillies, coriander and turmeric. Heat 30ml/2 tbsp of the oil in a heavy frying pan. Add the chipstick mixture and water. Cook until the chipsticks turn soft, and then crisp.

2 Place a dinner plate over the frying pan, and hold in place as you turn the pan over and carefully transfer the chipstick pancake on to the plate. Heat the remaining oil in the pan and slide the pancake back into the frying pan to brown the other side.

3 Gently break the eggs over the pancake, cover the frying pan and allow the eggs to set over a low heat. Season well and sprinkle with spring onions. Cook until the base is crisp. Serve hot for breakfast in the Parsi style, or with chapatis and a salad for lunch or supper.

STUFFED OKRA

The Gujarati community excels in the art of vegetarian cooking. Although some meat-and poultry-based dishes originated in Gujarat due to the presence of the Parsis, the native Gujaratis are strict vegetarians, who do not even eat eggs. Stuffed okra is easy to make and will happily accompany most meat and poultry dishes.

SERVES 4–6

225g/8oz large okra
15ml/1 tbsp amchur (dry
    mango powder)
2.5ml/½ tsp ground ginger
2.5ml/½ tsp ground cumin
2.5ml/½ tsp chilli powder
    (optional)
2.5ml/½ tsp ground turmeric
vegetable oil, for frying and mixing
30ml/2 tbsp cornflour (cornstarch),
    placed in a plastic bag
salt

1 Wash the okra and trim the tips. Make a slit lengthwise in the centre of each okra; do not cut all the way through.

2 In a bowl, mix the amchur, ginger, cumin, chilli, if using, turmeric and salt with a few drops of vegetable oil. Leave the mixture to rest for 1–2 hours or refrigerate overnight.

3 Using your fingers, part the slit of each okra carefully without opening it all the way and fill each with as much filling as possible. Put all the okra into the plastic bag with the cornflour and shake the bag carefully to cover the okra evenly.

4 Fill a wok, karahi or large pan with enough oil to sit 2.5cm/1in deep. Heat the oil and fry the okra in small batches for 5–8 minutes or until they are brown and slightly crisp. Serve hot with any meat, poultry or fish curry.

COOK'S TIP
When buying okra, choose one without any blemishes. Wash them thoroughly, rubbing each one gently with a soft vegetable brush or your fingertips.

OKRA in YOGURT

This tangy vegetable dish can be served as an accompaniment, but also makes an excellent vegetarian meal served with tarka dhal and chapatis. The secret of cooking okra is not to disturb its glutinous tendencies by overcooking, as the results can be unpleasant. Do follow the temperature and timing carefully.

SERVES 4

450g/1lb okra
30ml/2 tbsp vegetable oil
2.5ml/½ tsp onion seeds
3 fresh red or green chillies, chopped
1 onion, sliced
1.5ml/¼ tsp ground turmeric
10ml/2 tsp desiccated (dry, unsweetened, shredded) coconut
2.5ml/½ tsp salt
15ml/1 tbsp natural (plain) yogurt
2 tomatoes, quartered
15ml/1 tbsp chopped fresh coriander (cilantro)

1 Wash and trim the okra, cut into 1cm/½in pieces and set aside.

2 Heat the oil in a wok, karahi or large pan. Add the onion seeds, green chillies and onion, and fry for 5 minutes.

3 When the onion is golden brown, lower the heat and add the turmeric, desiccated coconut and salt. Fry for about 1 minute, stirring all the time.

4 Add the okra pieces to the pan. Turn the heat to medium-high and stir-fry briskly for a few minutes, until the okra has turned lightly golden.

5 Add the yogurt, tomatoes and fresh coriander. Cook for a further 2 minutes. Transfer to a warmed serving dish and serve immediately, as a side dish.

BOMBAY POTATO

This well-known dish is served in most Indian restaurants in the West, but it does not exist in Bombay. The origin of the name Bombay potato remains a mystery, although one theory is that it resembles a dish sold by street vendors in Bombay.

SERVES 4–6

450g/1lb whole new potatoes
5ml/1 tsp ground turmeric
60ml/4 tbsp vegetable oil
2 dried red chillies
6–8 curry leaves
2 onions, finely chopped
2 fresh green chillies, finely chopped
50g/2oz coarsely chopped fresh coriander
    (cilantro)
1.5ml/¼ tsp asafoetida
2.5ml/½ tsp each cumin, mustard,
    onion, fennel and nigella seeds
lemon juice, to taste
salt

1 Scrub the potatoes under running water and cut into small pieces. Boil the potatoes in water with a little salt and 2.5ml/½ tsp of the turmeric until tender. Drain well then coarsely mash. Set aside.

2 Heat the oil and fry the dried chillies and curry leaves until the chillies are nearly burnt. Add the onions, green chillies, coriander, remaining turmeric, asafoetida and spice seeds and cook until the onions are soft.

3 Fold in the potatoes and add a few drops of water. Cook gently over a low heat for 10 minutes, mixing well to ensure even distribution of the spices. Add lemon juice to taste.

4 Serve the potatoes with parathas or, as they would be eaten in Bombay, as a snack with soft white bread rolls.

CHICKPEAS with SPICED POTATO CAKES

This is a typical Bombay street snack; the kind that the Bombayites would happily eat while walking along the beach or watching a cricket match. It is the kind of food that brings together the cosmopolitan population of the city.

MAKES 10–12

30ml/2 tbsp vegetable oil
30ml/2 tbsp ground coriander
30ml/2 tbsp ground cumin
2.5ml/½ tsp ground turmeric
2.5ml/½ tsp salt
2.5ml/½ tsp granulated sugar
30ml/2 tbsp gram flour (besan), mixed
    with a little water to make a paste
450g/1lb/3 cups boiled chickpeas, drained
2 fresh green chillies, chopped
5cm/2in piece fresh root ginger, crushed
85g/3oz chopped fresh coriander
    (cilantro)
2 firm tomatoes, chopped
fresh mint sprigs, to garnish

For the potato cakes
450g/1lb potatoes, boiled and mashed
4 fresh green chillies, finely chopped
50g/2oz finely chopped fresh coriander
    (cilantro)
7.5ml/1½ tsp ground cumin
5ml/1 tsp amchur (dry mango powder)
vegetable oil, for shallow frying
salt

1 To prepare the chickpeas, heat the oil in a wok, karahi or large pan. Fry the coriander, cumin, turmeric, salt, sugar and gram flour paste until the water has evaporated and the oil has separated.

2 Add the chickpeas to the spices in the pan, and stir in the chopped chillies, ginger, fresh coriander and tomatoes. Toss the ingredients well and simmer gently for about 5 minutes. Transfer to a serving dish and keep warm.

3 To make the potato cakes, place the mashed potato in a large bowl and add the green chillies, chopped fresh coriander, cumin and amchur powder and salt. Mix together until all the ingredients are well blended.

4 Using your hands, shape the potato mixture into little cakes. Heat the oil in a shallow frying pan and fry the cakes on both sides until golden brown. Transfer to a serving dish, garnish with mint sprigs and serve with the chickpeas.

POTATOES in a YOGURT SAUCE

The potato was first introduced to India by Dutch traders, and it has since been elevated to gourmet status. In Indian cuisine, the humble potato takes on delicious flavourings of simple whole spices, or of blends of spices ground together.

SERVES 4

12 new potatoes, halved
300ml/½ pint/1¼ cups natural (plain) yogurt, whisked
300ml/½ pint/1¼ cups water
1.5ml/¼ tsp ground turmeric
5ml/1 tsp chilli powder
5ml/1 tsp ground coriander
2.5ml/½ tsp ground cumin
5ml/1 tsp salt
5ml/1 tsp soft brown sugar
30ml/2 tbsp vegetable oil
5ml/1 tsp cumin seeds
15ml/1 tbsp chopped fresh coriander (cilantro), plus extra sprigs to garnish (optional)
2 fresh green chillies, sliced

1 Boil the halved new potatoes with their skins on in a large pan of salted water, until they are just tender. Drain the potatoes and set aside.

2 Mix together the natural yogurt, water, turmeric, chilli powder, ground coriander, ground cumin, salt and sugar in a bowl. Set the mixture aside.

COOK'S TIPS
• If new potatoes are out of season and unavailable, you could use 450g/1lb ordinary potatoes instead. Peel and wash them and cut into large chunks, then cook as described above.
• Add 10ml/2 tsp gram flour (besan) to the yogurt to prevent it curdling.

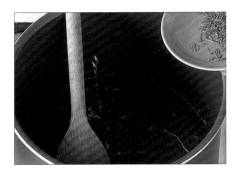

3 Heat the vegetable oil in a wok, karahi or large pan, and add the cumin seeds. Fry gently until they begin to splutter.

4 Reduce the heat, stir in the yogurt mixture and cook for about 3 minutes over a medium heat.

5 Add the chopped fresh coriander, green chillies and cooked potatoes. Blend everything together and cook for a further 5–7 minutes, stirring the mixture occasionally.

6 Transfer to a warmed serving dish and garnish with the coriander sprig, if you like. This dish goes very well with hot bhaturas or chapatis.

STUFFED VEGETABLES

It is hard to beat the Gujarati community when it comes to the creation of imaginative vegetarian dishes. In this fabulous recipe, two different vegetables are stuffed with an irresistible blend of spices and peanuts.

SERVES 4

12 small potatoes
8 baby aubergines (eggplant)
single (light) cream, to garnish

For the stuffing
15ml/1 tbsp sesame seeds
30ml/2 tbsp ground coriander
30ml/2 tbsp ground cumin
2.5ml/½ tsp salt
1.5ml/¼ tsp chilli powder
2.5ml/½ tsp ground turmeric
10ml/2 tsp granulated sugar
1.5ml/¼ tsp garam masala
15ml/1 tbsp peanuts, roughly crushed
15ml/1 tbsp gram flour (besan)
2 garlic cloves, crushed
15ml/1 tbsp lemon juice
30ml/2 tbsp chopped fresh coriander
    (cilantro)

For the sauce
30ml/2 tbsp vegetable oil
2.5ml/½ tsp black mustard seeds
400g/14oz can chopped tomatoes
30ml/2 tbsp chopped fresh coriander
    (cilantro)
150ml/¼ pint/⅔ cup water

1 Preheat the oven to 200°C/400°F/ Gas 6. Make slits in the potatoes and baby aubergines, making sure that you do not cut right through.

2 Mix all the ingredients for the stuffing together on a plate.

3 Carefully stuff the potatoes and aubergines with the spice mixture.

4 Place the potatoes and aubergines in a greased ovenproof dish.

5 Heat the oil in a pan and fry the mustard seeds for 2 minutes until they begin to splutter, then add the tomatoes, coriander and any leftover stuffing, together with the water. Simmer for 5 minutes until the sauce thickens.

6 Pour the sauce over the potatoes and aubergines. Cover and bake for 25–30 minutes until the vegetables are soft. Garnish with single cream, if using. Serve with any Indian bread or with a meat or chicken curry of your choice.

CHICKEN PULAO

Like biryanis, pulaos cooked with meat and poultry make a convenient one-pot meal.
A vegetable curry makes a good accompaniment, although for a simpler meal, such as
supper, you could serve the pulao with a simple raita, combining natural yogurt with
any raw vegetable, such as white cabbage, grated carrots, or cauliflower florets.

SERVES 4

400g/14oz/2 cups basmati rice
75g/3oz/6 tbsp ghee or unsalted
  (sweet) butter
1 onion, sliced
1.5ml/¼ tsp mixed onion and mustard
  seeds
3 curry leaves
5ml/1 tsp grated fresh root ginger
5ml/1 tsp crushed garlic
5ml/1 tsp ground coriander
5ml/1 tsp chilli powder
7.5ml/1½ tsp salt
2 tomatoes, sliced
1 potato, cubed
50g/2oz/½ cup frozen peas, thawed
175g/6oz chicken breast fillets, skinned
  and cubed
60ml/4 tbsp chopped fresh coriander
  (cilantro)
2 fresh green chillies, chopped
700ml/1¼ pints/3 cups water

1 Wash the rice thoroughly under
running water, then leave to soak for
30 minutes. Drain and set aside in a
sieve (strainer).

2 In a pan, melt the ghee or butter and
fry the sliced onion until golden.

3 Add the onion and mustard seeds,
the curry leaves, ginger, garlic, ground
coriander, chilli powder and salt. Stir-fry
for about 2 minutes over a low heat:
ground spices require only gentle
warmth to release their flavours.

4 Add the sliced tomatoes, cubed
potato, peas and chicken and mix
everything together well.

5 Add the rice and stir gently to
combine with the other ingredients.

6 Add the coriander and chillies. Mix
and stir-fry for 1 minute. Pour in the
water, bring to the boil and then lower
the heat. Cover and cook for 20 minutes.
Remove from the heat and leave the
pulao to stand for 6–8 minutes. Serve.

TRICOLOUR PULAO

Most Indian restaurants in the West serve this popular vegetable pulao, which has three different vegetables. The effect is easily achieved with canned or frozen vegetables, but for entertaining or a special occasion dinner, you may prefer to use fresh produce.

SERVES 4–6

225g/8oz/1 cup basmati rice, rinsed
   and soaked for 30 minutes
30ml/2 tbsp vegetable oil
2.5ml/½ tsp cumin seeds
2 dried bay leaves
4 green cardamom pods
4 cloves
1 onion, finely chopped
1 carrot, finely diced
50g/2oz/½ cup frozen peas, thawed
50g/2oz/⅓ cup frozen sweetcorn, thawed
25g/1oz/¼ cup cashew nuts, lightly fried
475ml/16fl oz/2 cups water
1.5ml/¼ tsp ground cumin
salt

1 Heat the oil in a wok, karahi or large pan over a medium heat, and fry the cumin seeds for 2 minutes. Add the bay leaves, cardamoms and cloves, and fry gently for 2 minutes more, stirring the spices from time to time.

2 Add the onion and fry until lightly browned. Stir in the diced carrot and cook, stirring, for 3–4 minutes.

3 Drain the soaked basmati rice and add to the contents in the pan. Stir well to mix. Add the peas, sweetcorn and fried cashew nuts.

4 Add the measured water and the remaining spices, and add salt to taste. Bring to the boil, cover and simmer for 15 minutes over a low heat until all the water is absorbed.

5 Leave to stand, covered, for 10 minutes. Transfer to a warmed dish and serve.

PRAWN BIRYANI

The recipe for biryani originated with mutton, but its popularity has tempted Indian chefs to create versions using other ingredients. As with all biryanis, this one using prawns is a meal in itself. The classic accompaniment to any biryani is a raita.

SERVES 4–6

2 large onions, finely sliced and
   deep-fried
300ml/½ pint/1¼ cups natural
   (plain) yogurt
30ml/2 tbsp tomato purée (paste)
60ml/4 tbsp green masala paste
30ml/2 tbsp lemon juice
5ml/1 tsp black cumin seeds
5cm/2in piece cinnamon stick, or
   1.5ml/¼ tsp ground cinnamon
4 green cardamom pods
450g/1lb raw king prawns (jumbo
   shrimp), peeled and deveined
225g/8oz/3 cups small whole button
   (white) mushrooms
225g/8oz/2 cups frozen peas, thawed
450g/1lb/2⅓ cups basmati rice,
   soaked for 5 minutes in boiled
   water and drained
300ml/½ pint/1¼ cups water
1 sachet saffron powder, mixed in
   90ml/6 tbsp milk
30ml/2 tbsp ghee or unsalted (sweet)
   butter
salt

1 In a bowl, mix the onions, yogurt, tomato purée, masala paste, lemon juice, cumin seeds, cinnamon and cardamom, with salt to taste. Fold in the prawns, mushrooms and peas. Leave for 2 hours. Preheat the oven to 190°C/375°F/Gas 5.

2 Grease the base of a heavy pan and add the prawns, vegetables and any marinade juices. Cover with the drained rice and smooth the surface gently until you have an even layer.

3 Pour the water over the surface of the rice. Make holes through the rice with the handle of a spoon and pour into each a little saffron milk. Place knobs (pats) of ghee or butter on the surface.

4 Place a circular piece of foil on top of the rice. Cover and cook in the oven for 45–50 minutes. Allow to stand for 8–10 minutes, then stir the biryani and serve hot.

TOMATO and SPINACH PULAO

A tasty and nourishing dish for vegetarians and meat eaters alike. Serve it with another vegetable curry, or with tandoori chicken, marinated fried fish or shammi kabab. Add a cooling fruit raita for a completely balanced meal.

2 Drain the rice, add it to the pan and cook for a further 1–2 minutes, stirring, until the rice is coated.

3 Stir in the dhana jeera powder or coriander and cumin, then add the carrots. Season with salt and pepper. Pour in the stock and stir well to mix.

SERVES 4

30ml/2 tbsp vegetable oil
15ml/1 tbsp ghee or unsalted (sweet)
   butter
1 onion, chopped
2 garlic cloves, crushed
3 tomatoes, peeled, seeded and chopped
225g/8oz/generous 1 cup brown basmati
   rice, soaked
10ml/2 tsp dhana jeera powder or
   5ml/1 tsp ground coriander and
   5ml/1 tsp ground cumin
2 carrots, coarsely grated
900ml/1½ pints/3¾ cups vegetable stock
275g/10oz young spinach leaves
50g/2oz/½ cup unsalted cashew nuts,
   toasted
salt and ground black pepper
naan bread, to serve

1 Heat the oil and ghee or butter in a wok, karahi or large pan, and fry the onion and garlic for 4–5 minutes until soft. Add the tomatoes and cook for 3–4 minutes, stirring, until thickened.

COOK'S TIP
Leaving to rest for 6–8 minutes before serving makes the rice dry and fluffy.

4 Bring to the boil, then cover tightly and simmer over a very gentle heat for 20–25 minutes, until the rice is tender. Lay the spinach on the surface of the rice, cover again, and cook for a further 2–3 minutes, until the spinach has wilted. Fold the spinach into the rest of the rice and check the seasoning. Sprinkle with toasted cashews and serve with naan.

CHICKEN BIRYANI

Biryani is a meal in itself and needs no accompaniment, except for a raita and some grilled or fried poppadums. It is a dish that is equally at home on the family dining table or as a dinner-party centrepiece.

SERVES 4

10 whole green cardamom pods
275g/10oz/1½ cups basmati rice, soaked
    and drained
2.5ml/½ tsp salt
2–3 whole cloves
5cm/2in piece cinnamon stick
45ml/3 tbsp vegetable oil
3 onions, sliced
4 chicken breast fillets, each about 175g/
    6oz, skinned and cubed
1.5ml/¼ tsp ground cloves
1.5ml/¼ tsp hot chilli powder
5ml/1 tsp ground cumin
5ml/1 tsp ground coriander
2.5ml/½ tsp ground black pepper
3 garlic cloves, chopped
5ml/1 tsp finely chopped fresh root ginger
juice of 1 lemon
4 tomatoes, sliced
30ml/2 tbsp chopped fresh coriander
    (cilantro)
150ml/¼ pint/⅔ cup natural (plain) yogurt,
    plus extra to serve
4–5 saffron threads, soaked in 10ml/2 tsp
    warm milk
150ml/¼ pint/⅔ cup water
toasted flaked (sliced) almonds and fresh
    coriander (cilantro) sprigs, to garnish

1 Preheat the oven to 190°C/375°F/
Gas 5. Remove the seeds from half the
cardamom pods and grind them finely,
using a pestle and mortar. Set aside the
ground seeds.

2 Bring a pan of water to the boil and
add the rice, salt, whole cardamom
pods, cloves and cinnamon stick. Boil for
2 minutes, then drain, leaving the whole
spices in the rice. Keep the rice hot in
a covered pan.

3 Heat the oil in a wok, karahi or large
pan, and fry the onions for 8 minutes,
until softened and browned. Add the
chicken and the ground spices, including
the ground cardamom seeds. Mix well,
then add the garlic, ginger and lemon
juice. Stir-fry for about 5 minutes.

4 Transfer the chicken mixture to a
casserole and arrange the tomatoes
on top. Sprinkle on the fresh coriander,
spoon the yogurt evenly on top and
cover with the drained rice.

5 Drizzle the saffron milk over the rice
and pour over the water. Cover, then
bake for 1 hour. Transfer to a serving
platter and discard the whole spices.
Garnish and serve immediately.

BEEF BIRYANI

This biryani, which uses beef, is a speciality of the Muslim community. The recipe may seem long, but biryani is one of the easiest and most relaxing ways of cooking, especially when you are entertaining. Once the dish is assembled and placed in the oven, it looks after itself and you can happily get on with other things.

SERVES 4

2 large onions
2 garlic cloves, chopped
2.5cm/1in piece of fresh root ginger,
    peeled and roughly chopped
½–1 fresh green chilli, seeded and chopped
small bunch of fresh coriander (cilantro)
60ml/4 tbsp flaked (sliced) almonds
30–45ml/2–3 tbsp water
15ml/1 tbsp ghee or butter, plus
    25g/1oz/2 tbsp butter for the rice
45ml/3 tbsp vegetable oil
30ml/2 tbsp sultanas (golden raisins)
500g/1¼lb braising or stewing steak,
    cubed
5ml/1 tsp ground coriander
15ml/1 tbsp ground cumin
2.5ml/½ tsp ground turmeric
2.5ml/½ tsp ground fenugreek
good pinch of ground cinnamon
175ml/6fl oz/¾ cup natural (plain)
    yogurt, whisked
275g/10oz/1½ cups basmati rice
about 1.2 litres/2 pints/5 cups hot
    chicken stock or water
salt and ground black pepper
2 hard-boiled (hard-cooked) eggs,
    quartered, to garnish
chapatis, to serve

1 Roughly chop one onion and place it in a food processor or blender. Add the garlic, ginger, chilli, fresh coriander and half the flaked almonds. Pour in the water and process to a smooth paste. Transfer the paste to a small bowl and set aside.

2 Finely slice the remaining onion into rings or half rings. Heat half the ghee or butter with half the oil in a heavy flameproof casserole and fry the onion rings for 10–15 minutes until they are a deep golden brown. Transfer to a plate with a slotted spoon. Fry the remaining flaked almonds briefly until golden and set aside with the onion rings, then quickly fry the sultanas until they swell. Transfer to the plate.

3 Heat the remaining ghee or butter in the casserole with a further 15ml/1 tbsp of the oil. Fry the cubed meat, in batches, until evenly browned on all sides. Transfer the meat to a plate and set aside.

4 Wipe the casserole clean with kitchen paper, heat the remaining oil and pour in the onion, spice and coriander paste made earlier. Cook over a medium heat for 2–3 minutes, stirring all the time, until the mixture begins to brown lightly. Stir in all the additional spices, season with salt and ground black pepper and cook for 1 minute more.

5 Lower the heat, then stir in the yogurt, a little at a time. When all of it has been incorporated into the spice mixture, return the meat to the casserole. Stir to coat, cover tightly and simmer over a gentle heat for 40–45 minutes until the meat is tender. Meanwhile, soak the rice in a bowl of cold water for 15–20 minutes.

6 Preheat the oven to 160°C/325°F/Gas 3. Drain the rice, place in a pan and add the hot chicken stock or water, together with a little salt. Bring back to the boil, cover and cook for 5 minutes.

7 Drain the rice, and pile it in a mound on top of the meat in the casserole. Using the handle of a spoon, make a hole through the rice and meat mixture, to the bottom of the pan. Place the fried onions, almonds and sultanas over the top and dot with butter. Cover the casserole tightly with a double layer of foil and secure with a lid.

8 Cook the biryani in the preheated oven for 30–40 minutes. To serve, spoon the mixture on to a warmed serving platter and garnish with the quartered hard-boiled eggs. Serve with chapatis.

COOK'S TIP
Place a piece of buttered greaseproof (waxed) paper on the rice. This will help to keep the top layer moist in the oven.

CHAPATIS

A chapati is an unleavened bread made from chapati flour, a ground wholemeal flour known as atta, which is finer than the Western equivalent. An equal quantity of standard wholemeal flour and plain flour will also produce satisfactory results, although chapati flour is available from Indian grocers. This is the everyday bread of the Indian home.

MAKES 8–10

225g/8oz/2 cups chapati flour or ground
   wholemeal (whole-wheat) flour
2.5ml/½ tsp salt
175ml/6fl oz/¾ cup water

1 Place the flour and salt in a mixing bowl. Make a well in the middle and gradually stir in the water, mixing well with your fingers. Form a supple dough and knead for 7–10 minutes. Ideally, cover with clear film and leave on one side for 15–20 minutes to rest.

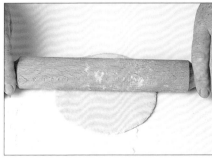

2 Divide the dough into 8–10 equal portions. Roll out each piece in a circle on a well-floured surface.

3 Place a *tava* (chapati griddle) or heavy frying pan over a high heat. When steam rises from it, lower the heat to medium and add the first chapati to the pan.

4 When the chapati begins to bubble, turn it over. Press down with a clean dish towel or a flat spoon and turn once again. Remove the cooked chapati from the pan and keep warm in a piece of foil lined with kitchen paper while you cook the other chapatis. Repeat the process until all the breads are cooked. Serve the chapatis immediately.

BHATURAS

These leavened and deep-fried breads are from Punjab, where the local people enjoy them with a bowl of spicy chickpea curry. The combination has become a classic over the years and is known as choley bhature. *Bhaturas must be eaten hot and cannot be reheated.*

MAKES 10 BHATURAS

15g/½oz fresh yeast
5ml/1 tsp granulated sugar
120ml/4fl oz/½ cup lukewarm water
200g/7oz/1¾ cups plain (all-purpose) flour
50g/2oz/½ cup semolina
2.5ml/½ tsp salt
15g/½oz/1 tbsp ghee or butter
30ml/2 tbsp natural (plain) yogurt
oil, for frying

COOK'S TIP

Ghee is availabe from Indian stores and some supermarkets. However, it is easy to make at home. Melt unsalted (sweet) butter over a low heat. Simmer very gently until the residue becomes light golden, then leave to cool. Strain through muslin (cheesecloth) before using.

1 Mix the yeast with the sugar and water in a jug (pitcher). Sift the flour into a large bowl and stir in the semolina and salt. Rub in the butter or ghee.

2 Add the yeast mixture and yogurt and mix to a dough. Turn out on to a lightly floured surface and knead for 10 minutes until smooth and elastic.

3 Place the dough in an oiled bowl, cover with oiled clear film (plastic wrap) and leave to rise, in a warm place, for about 1 hour, or until doubled in size.

4 Turn out on to a lightly floured surface and knock back (punch down). Divide into ten equal pieces and shape each into a ball. Flatten into discs with the palm of your hand. Roll out on a lightly floured surface into 13cm/5in rounds.

5 Heat oil to a depth of 1cm/½in in a deep frying pan and slide one bhatura into the oil. Fry for about 1 minute, turning over after 30 seconds, then drain well on kitchen paper. Keep each bhatura warm in a low oven while frying the remaining bhaturas. Serve immediately, while hot.

REGIONAL DIVERSITY

The food culture of South-east Asia varies widely across the region, with each country following its own long-standing traditions for spice blends, flavourings and cooking styles. However, there are also many similarities, largely because of the trade in ingredients, the influences of climate, geography and religion, and of powerful neighbouring countries, such as China.

Thailand

Between Burma and Vietnam lies Thailand, the only country in South-east Asia that has never been colonized by European powers. The word *thai* means free, and the people of Thailand are proud of their independence. In terms of size, Thailand is roughly equal to Burma, but smaller than both India and China. It is divided into five regions, each with its own distinctive geography and culture.

Bangkok, the capital of Thailand, is popularly known as the Venice of the East, because the city is built around

Below: The South-east Asian region covers a multitude of countries, all quite individual.

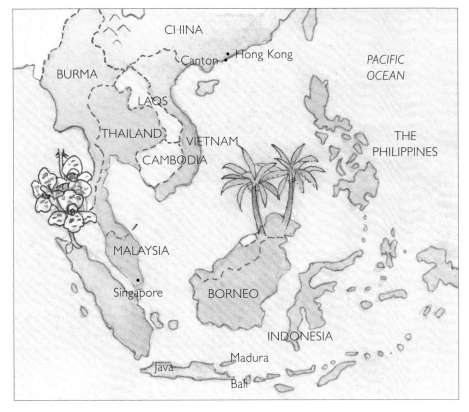

Above: A Thai hod market, so named because farmers display their produce in open baskets, which they carry to market on the ends of long poles, known as hods.

extensive inland waterways, and the majority of the city's population lives along the numerous canals. The floating markets are the workplace of a vast number of people, who sell fruits and vegetables, chillies, fresh fish and a wealth of other exotic ingredients. Thailand is renowned for its excellence in the art of fruit and vegetable carving, and an enjoyable day can be spent watching the various demonstrations on the streets of Bangkok.

Buddhism is the religion of Thailand, although most people seem to have a fairly liberal attitude to Buddhist law, and Thai cuisine includes an extensive range of meat-based recipes. It is fish, shellfish and vegetables, however, that constitute the main part of the Thai diet. Salads are central to a Thai meal, and there are many varieties made, some of which use exotic fruits such as mangoes, pineapple and papaya, as well as raw vegetables. A small quantity of shredded meat, such as pork, is sometimes added, perhaps with perhaps a few prawns (shrimp). Thai salad dressings are a delicious blend of fish sauce, brown sugar and lime juice.

The particular climate conditions and geographical position of Thailand have given rise to regional variations in the nation's cuisine. In southern Thailand, the Gulf of Thailand and the Andaman Sea provide a wealth of fish and shellfish. Dishes based on these ingredients are popular throughout the country, but are particularly important in the south. In the north, where the climate is slightly cooler, fruits such as lychees are grown in abundance. Chicken, fish and glutinous rice are eaten in the north-east.

Coconut plays a very important role in Thai cooking. Coconut milk, flavoured

with ginger, lemon grass, pungent local chillies and basil leaves, forms the basis of most Thai curries. Many desserts are also made using coconut milk and palm sugar. Whatever the dish, there is always a fine balance and complexity of flavour, texture and colour. Thai people regard food as a celebration, and it is considered bad luck to eat alone.

Burma

Colonized by the British in the late 19th century, Burma finally gained its independence in 1948, after a politically turbulent period, one year after the end of British rule in India. The country was officially renamed Myanmar in 1989. The national religion of Burma is Buddhism, which, like Hinduism, forbids

Below: The lively and colourful floating markets on the waterways of Burma sell supplies of fresh fish, fruits and vegetables.

the taking of another life for reasons of personal gratification. Although strict followers observe this rule, in practice most people eat a fair amount of meat, and fish is even more popular: Mohingha (Burmese Fish Stew) is flavoured with Indian spices, and is almost the national dish. Burmese food has noticeable Indian and Chinese influences. Spices from India are often sold in the local street markets, although the country's cuisine generally has more subtle flavours than its Indian counterpart. Rice is the staple food, but noodles, a Chinese contribution, are also very popular. The use of groundnut (peanut) oil and coconut suggests an Indian influence, whereas sesame oil, which is also used as a cooking medium, is a distinctly Chinese ingredient.

Vietnam

Lying virtually next door to Thailand, Vietnam has a cuisine that is in a class of its own. The country was ruled by the French for nearly 80 years, and a French culinary influence can still be detected. The most prominent influence, however, is that of the Chinese, who occupied Vietnam for nearly a thousand years.

Vietnamese food is light and delicate, and the use of fat is limited. Generally speaking, the Vietnamese prefer spicy food, with a well-balanced flavour and a clean taste. Rice and noodles are once again the staples, as in other South-east Asian countries. Plenty of fresh fruit and vegetables are consumed, along with small quantities of meat, and fish and shellfish feature high on the menus.

Malaysia

Bordering Thailand in the north and Indonesia in the south, Malaysia is a lush, tropical land, with widely varying landscapes. It has a genuine diversity of races and cultures, and this is reflected in the country's varied cuisine. Navigation is easy throughout this area, and people have long been able to exchange cooking styles and ingredients with neighbouring countries.

The culinary heritage of Malaysia reaches back for at least six centuries, when the country began to attract

between southern Indian and Malaysian cooking, with only minor differences, such as the use of lime leaves in Malaysian cooking and curry leaves in south Indian.

The tremendous variety in Malaysian cuisine is also partly a result of the range of religious beliefs within the country. For example, no pork is eaten among the Muslim community, although pork is a particular favourite of the Chinese. The Hindus from India will not eat beef, whereas the local Malay population has excellent beef-based recipes. Dishes such as rendang and sambal, which suggest an Indonesian influence, exist side by side with biryanis and samosas, which are unmistakably Indian. The Malaysian dessert *gula melaka* is a superb local creation, which is made with sago, enriched with thick coconut milk and sweetened with palm sugar with a touch of spices.

Indonesia

Comprising 13,000 islands spread along the Indian Ocean, Indonesia is a lush, green fertile land with steamy tropical heat and snow-capped mountain peaks.

For over two thousand years, waves of foreign traders and merchants entered the islands, and Hindu, Muslim

traders and travellers from far-flung places. India and Arabia were the first to exploit the country for its precious goods, followed by the Chinese and Portuguese. Trading began in such commodities as raw silk, brocades, fine silver and pearls, which were exchanged for peppercorns (known as black gold in those days), cloves, nutmeg and mace. Chinese princesses were sent by the emperor as gifts for the Malay sultan. Many Chinese men came to Malaysia to find work, married local women and settled in the country. This started a culture of Chinese food in Malaysia, to which the local people added their own touch. A new style of cuisine was thus created, which had Chinese influences, but flavours that were essentially local.

Above: A street stall in Singapore. One of the strongest influences on Malay cuisine has come from Chinese migrant workers.

Right: A typical Indonesian farmhouse on the island of Java. Green vegetables grow well in this lush tropical climate.

Southern India has also had an impact on Malaysian cooking, as Indian workers from the south were hired to work in the rubber plantations in Malacca. There are striking resemblances evident

Above: Local fishermen leave freshly caught mackerel to dry in the hot midday sun on the beaches of Bali, Indonesia.

on the cuisine of the country. The most significant influences on eating habits undoubtably came from the Hindus and Muslims, and the Chinese.

In no other South-east Asian country does rice play such a major role as in Indonesia. It is eaten twice a day with numerous types of curry. On the island of Bali, Hindus eat rice with fish curries, Muslims eat it with beef and chicken, and the Chinese eat it with almost any meat, including duck. The famous Indonesian style of serving a meal, known as *nasi gerai* (loosely translated as the rice table), was even popular with the Dutch. *Nasi* means rice and *gerar* refers to the endless variety of other dishes served with it. Nasi Goreng (fried rice) is one of the best-known dishes, along with Gado Gado, a cooked vegetable salad with a delicious peanut dressing. Beef Rendang, with the pungency of chillies and ginger, the warmth of cumin and the sweet, mellow flavour of coconut milk, is one of Indonesia's most enduring dishes.

The Philippines

Like that of its neighbours, Filipino cooking is a harmonious blend of the cuisine of many countries and cultures. There are notable similarities with other South-east Asian countries, in terms of the way that ingredients are grown, prepared and cooked.

The original Filipinos are believed to have been of Malayo-Polynesian origin, but the age of discovery and exploitation brought traders from many neighbouring countries, including China, Malaysia, Japan and Indonesia. However, the strongest influence came from the Spanish, who arrived in the 16th century. They ruled the country for nearly 400 years, and during that time they established Christianity, making the Philippines the only Asian country with the Christian faith. Filipinos love both siestas and fiestas, which are both legacies from the Spanish. Dishes such as Bombonese Arroz (rice fritters), Arroz Caldo (rice with chicken) and Puchero (a mixed meat soup) are among the more popular Spanish-influenced dishes still eaten

and Buddhist kingdoms have all been established and destroyed. The Hindus in the 1st century, and the Buddhists in the 8th, established a vegetarian ethos, based on their own strict religious beliefs. Arab traders introduced Islam in the 15th century, and even today the Muslim community in Indonesia does not eat pork. Along with the Arabs, the Indians and Chinese were the first traders to visit Indonesia, lured by its spices, and by nutmeg, mace and cloves, in particular. Arab traders took shiploads of these spices into Europe and sold them at highly inflated prices.

The Europeans soon saw the benefit of eliminating the middle man, and the Portuguese, Dutch, English and Spanish all began sailing to Indonesia themselves, referring to the islands as the Spice

Islands of the East. The Portuguese and British set up trading posts, but the Dutch eventually colonized Indonesia, and they stayed for 250 years, until the country gained independence in 1945. Throughout the period of Dutch rule, Chinese migrants, traders and workers continued to add their own distinctive traditions to the already rich tapestry of Indonesian culture.

With such diverse cultural influences, Indonesian cuisine emerged as one of the most varied and interesting in the whole of South-east Asia. Yet, although Indonesia was a Dutch colony, the Dutch themselves have had very little impact

Above: Rice is the principal crop grown on the intricately terraced fields in the Luzon region of the Philippines. These terraces will provide employment for all inhabitants of the immediate area.

today. Before the arrival of the Spanish, the Americans came to the area, and together these two influences helped to make Filipino cuisine a harmonious blend of Eastern and Western styles.

Chinese influence was also strong in the area, and this is clearly evident from the endless variety of noodle-based dishes. Pansit Guisado (Noodles with Chicken, Prawns and Ham) is just one of a number of popular Chinese-inspired dishes. Rice is the staple food of the Philippines, however, and it is eaten daily with almost every meal, even breakfast. The everyday diet of Filipinos is based on a simple dish of rice, stir-fried with meat, fish and vegetables.

Adobo, a Filipino spicy stew made with pork, chicken or even fish and shellfish, is a real speciality of the islands. The sauce in which the ingredients are cooked is an irresistible blend of flavours, combining the tartness of local palm vinegar with the spiciness of black peppercorns and the unmistakable, pungent flavour of garlic. Although it owes much to Spanish origins, the dish, like so much of Filipino food, has its own distinctive character.

Left: Fishermen prepare to haul up their nets on the Calamian Islands, in the Philippines. The boat is known as a banca.

PRINCIPLES of SOUTH-EAST ASIAN COOKING

Food takes centre stage in the daily life of most people in South-east Asian. It is a well-known fact that food brings people together, and nowhere is this more apparent than across the Asian region. Food is one of life's greatest pleasures, and sharing it with family and friends is fundamental to the cultures of these countries. Quite simply, they live to eat.

All over South-east Asia, food is prepared with great attention to detail, using only the freshest ingredients. Dishes are healthy and easy to cook, with enough visual appeal to tempt anyone. Until fairly recently, recipes were not written down, but were handed down from generation to generation. The lack of written recipes has encouraged cooks to use their imagination when creating dishes, to experiment with flavours, while keeping to the principles of their local cooking styles and techniques.

Spices and aromatics

South-east Asian cooks are skilled in the art of combining spices, which they use to add taste, colour and aroma.

The essential spices of South-east Asia are coriander, cumin, turmeric, chilli and peppercorns, and although the same spices are used in India, the curries of South-east Asia are quite different, with a milder heat and more subtle flavours.

As in India, South-east Asian cuisine also makes use of whole spices, which are removed at the end of cooking. These include cinnamon, cloves and cardamom pods, and they are especially popular in Malaysia, where the influence of Indian cuisine is most strongly felt.

Adding flavour

Spice blends are usually combined with coconut milk, the most commonly used ingredient, and other hallmark ingredients, such as lemon grass and kaffir lime leaves. Most South-east Asian curries have a distinctive tangy taste, which comes from tamarind, the souring agent that is characteristic of all Asian cooking. Lime juice and vinegar are also used, and these add a refreshing tartness to curries, while the addition of soy sauce, fish sauce or shrimp paste gives that particular depth and pungent flavour that is so distinctive to South-east Asian cuisine. Among the fresh ingredients used as flavouring agents are shallots, galangal, ginger, garlic and chilli, as well as an array of fresh herbs, especially coriander (cilantro), mint and basil.

Below: Each country in South-east Asia has its own individual cooking style, but the essential approach to eating is the same: food is always fresh, full of flavour and carefully prepared and presented.

PREPARING a SOUTH-EAST ASIAN CURRY

Despite the many regional variations, South-east Asian curries are prepared following the same basic pattern. The differences in the cuisines can be attributed more to culture, lifestyle and local food resources, than to alternative cooking techniques.

Basic ingredients

The first point to consider when making any curry is what cooking medium to use. Coconut and palm oil are widely used throughout South-east Asia, and people in some countries, such as Thailand and the Philippines, use lard. To avoid consuming too much saturated fat, use a lighter cooking oil, such as vegetable oil or sunflower oil.

In South-east Asia, stock is more frequently used than water when making curries. This is probably because meat and poultry are cut into small pieces and are generally cooked off the bone. Stock adds an extra depth of flavour.

For thickening sauces, the common practice is to rely on ingredients such as coconut milk, grated coconut, onions, grated fresh root ginger and crushed garlic. In all curries, colour and pungency are created by the addition of different types of chillies, in varying amounts.

Cooking a curry

The starting point when making a curry is to preheat the oil and fry the onions, which, along with garlic and ginger, are the basic ingredients of all South-east Asian curries. Sometimes the onions are fried until they are crisp before the garlic and ginger are added, while in other dishes they are simply softened. The spices or curry paste are then added and cooked for a short time to eliminate their raw flavour. When the spices are cooked to the right point, the oil begins to separate from the thick spice paste.

By using a wide range of cooking techniques, a variety of flavours can be created from the same basic ingredients: recipes such as Beef Rendang and Thai Mussaman Curry are good examples of this. Although a recipe should initially be used as a guide, it is much more fun to be able to stamp your own personality

Above: Spices and aromatics can be used in many ways, and different flavours can be created from the same ingredients.

on to whatever you are cooking. This becomes easier with practice, and, after a while, using spices to prepare delicious South-east Asian curries becomes a work of art. Start to use spices as an artist uses a palette, as you tone and colour the food to your own taste.

Planning and serving

Dishes served at a South-east Asian meal are not categorized into separate courses, but are all brought to the table at the same time. Diners help themselves with many helpings of small quantities.

Rice is the cornerstone of all meals, and is served with one or two vegetable side dishes, relishes (such as different types of sambal), salads and curries. It is customary to serve more than one meat or poultry dish, a vegetable curry and a dry, spiced, stir-fried vegetable dish. A soup is another important part of a South-east Asian meal. Desserts are not generally served, except in Malaysia, where delicious hot and cold rice or sago desserts are cooked in coconut milk, sweetened with palm sugar.

Freezing foods

South-east Asian dishes are prepared very quickly, as meat and vegetables are cut into small pieces so that they can be stir-fried, and they are not marinated before cooking. As time-saving strategies, therefore, chilling and freezing are probably not as important in South-east Asian cuisine as they are to some other types of cooking. However, curries always taste better if they are cooked a day or two in advance. The spices seem to permeate the meat and poultry, and the final flavour is much more mellow.

If you plan to freeze the food you are cooking, the following basic guidelines may be helpful:
• Leave the food slightly underdone.
• Cool the food rapidly. The best way to do this is to tip it into a large tray (a large roasting pan is ideal) and leave it in a cool place.
• Once the food has cooled down, put it into appropriate containers, then label and chill it before finally putting it in the freezer. The food will keep in the freezer for 6–8 months, depending on the star rating of your freezer.
• Food from unplanned freezing, such as leftovers, should not be frozen for longer than 2–3 months.

DRY-FRYING WHOLE SPICES

Many whole spices benefit from being dry-fried before they are ground. This makes sure that no surface moisture remains, and it heightens and develops the flavour. To dry-fry spices, heat a wok or heavy pan for 1 minute, then add the spices. Cook for 2–3 minutes, stirring and shaking the pan constantly to prevent the spices from scorching. When the spices start to give off a warm, rich aroma, remove the pan from the heat and tip the spices into a spice mill or a mortar, and process or grind with a pestle. Purists recommend that each spice is dry-fried separately, but several spices can be cooked together, if watched over closely. All spices react differently to heat, so follow these basic guidelines for best results:

• Coriander seeds often provide the dominant flavour, especially in powders from Southern India and Singapore. Shake the pan well to keep the seeds on the move, and remove them from the heat when they start to give off a mild, sweet, orangey perfume.

• Dried chillies can be roasted in a cool oven, but it is better to sear them in a heavy pan, where you can keep an eye on them. Place the pan over a medium heat for 2–3 minutes, until the chillies soften and puff up. Do not let them burn, or the flavour will be ruined. Transfer to a plate immediately to stop them overheating or burning.

• Cumin seeds should be dry-fried in a pan, and will be ready for grinding when the seeds release their aroma, usually within 40–50 seconds.

• Black peppercorns need gentle dry-frying, just to heighten the flavour.

• Fenugreek needs to be watched carefully as it will become bitter if it is dry-fried for too long. It is ready when it turns brownish yellow.

• Curry leaves can be dry-fried over a cool to medium heat when fresh. Grind or pound them, using a mortar and pestle, to release their characteristic flavour, then mix them with the other spices. This works well if you are making a curry powder or paste that is to be used immediately, but if it is to be kept for more than 24 hours, make up the powder, then add the whole fresh or frozen leaves just before you are ready to use it. Remove the leaves before serving the curry. Avoid using dried curry leaves if possible, as they will have lost most of their flavour in the dehydration process.

Right: From top, compressed tamarind, compressed tamarind block and dried tamarind slices

Tamarind

Although tamarind doesn't have much of an aroma, its flavour is tart, sour, fruity and refreshing. It is used in many South-east Asian curries, chutneys and dhals, and is an essential ingredient of Thai hot and sour soups. Blocks of compressed tamarind and slices of dried tamarind have been available for a while, but it is now also possible to buy jars of fresh tamarind and cartons of tamarind concentrate and paste, which require less preparation time. There really is no substitute for tamarind. Some recipes may suggest using vinegar or lemon or lime juice instead, but the results will not compare with using the real thing.

Compressed tamarind is sold in a solid block and looks rather like dried dates.

To prepare it, tear off a piece that is roughly equivalent to 15ml/1 tbsp and soak it in 150ml/¼ pint/⅔ cup warm water for 10 minutes. Swirl the tamarind around with your fingers so that the pulp is released from the seeds. Using a nylon sieve, strain the juice into a jug (pitcher). Discard the contents of the sieve and use the liquid as required.

Tamarind slices look a little like dried apple slices. Place them in a small bowl, then pour over enough warm water to cover and leave to soak for 30 minutes to extract the flavour, squeeze the tamarind slices with your fingers, then strain the juice into a jug.

Tamarind concentrate or paste is sold in Asian food stores, and is a quick and convenient alternative to compressed

tamarind and tamarind slices. To prepare, mix 15ml/1 tbsp concentrate or paste with 60–90ml/4–6 tbsp warm water. Stir briskly until dissolved, then use as required in the recipe. Any leftover liquid can be stored in the refrigerator and used for another recipe.

CURRY POWDERS and PASTES

Curry powders and pastes are spice blends that are used as the basis of a curry. Traditionally, these mixtures would be prepared as needed, using fresh ingredients, but for convenience a wide variety of prepared pastes and powders are now available commercially, and most supermarket shelves carry a wealth of different spice mixtures from all parts of the globe. However, for enthusiastic cooks it is fun and a creative challenge to make up your own curry powders and pastes. Keep experimenting until you find the balance of spicing that suits you and your family. It is perfectly possible to mix ground spices, but it is more satisfying (and much more satisfactory in terms of flavour) to start with whole spices.

Curry powders

The word curry evolved from the Tamil word *kaari*, meaning any food cooked in a sauce. There is little doubt that curry powder, a ready-made blend of spices, was an early convenience food, prepared for merchants, sailors and military men who had served in the East and wished to bring these exotic flavours home.

Simple curry powder

This Malayan Chinese spice mixture is good for poultry, especially chicken, and robust fish curries.

MAKES ABOUT 60ML/4 TBSP

2 dried red chillies
6 whole cloves
1 small cinnamon stick
5ml/1 tsp coriander seeds
5ml/1 tsp fennel seeds
10ml/2 tsp Sichuan peppercorns
2.5ml/½ tsp freshly grated nutmeg
5ml/1 tsp ground star anise
5ml/1 tsp ground turmeric

WATCHPOINTS

• Ensure that you wash your hands, and the chopping board and other utensils thoroughly after preparing chillies.
• If your skin is particularly sensitive, then you should wear rubber gloves while you are preparing the chillies.

1 Remove the seeds from the dried chillies using the point of a knife, and discard any stems. If you prefer a very hot and punchy spice mixture, then retain some or all of the chilli seeds.

2 Put the chillies, cloves, cinnamon, coriander, fennel seeds and Sichuan peppercorns in a wok or large pan. Dry-fry the spices, tossing them around the pan frequently until they start to release a rich, spicy aroma.

3 Grind the spices to a smooth powder in a mortar, using a pestle. Alternatively, use a spice mill, or an electric coffee grinder that is reserved for the purpose.

4 Add the grated nutmeg, star anise and turmeric. Use immediately or store in an airtight jar away from strong light.

SEVEN-SEAS CURRY POWDER

Seven-seas Curry Powder is a mild spice blend used in Indonesian and Malaysian curries. The name refers to the seven seas, including the Andaman and South China Sea, that converge on the shores of Malaysia and the islands of Indonesia.

To make the powder, bruise 6–8 cardamom pods and put them in a wok with 90ml/6 tbsp coriander seeds, 45ml/3 tbsp cumin seeds, 22.5ml/1½ tbsp celery seeds, 5cm/2in piece cinnamon stick, 6–8 cloves and 15ml/1 tbsp chilli powder. Dry-fry until the rich aroma is released.

Curry pastes

On market stalls throughout South-east Asia are mounds of pounded wet spices: lemon grass, chilli, ginger, garlic, galangal, shallots and tamarind. After purchasing meat, chicken or fish, all the cook has to do is to call on the spice seller. He or she will ask a few questions: "What sort of curry is it to be? Hot or mild? How many servings?" Having ascertained the answers and perhaps exchanged a few more pleasantries, the appropriate quantities of each spice will be scooped on to a banana leaf and folded into a neat cone, ready to be taken home.

We may not be able to buy our ingredients in such colourful surroundings, but Western supermarkets now stock some very good ready-made pastes, or you can make your own at home. By experimenting, you will find the balance of flavours you like, and can then make your favourite mixtures in bulk. Store surplus curry paste in in the freezer.

COOK'S TIP

If you grind wet spices a lot, you may find it useful to invest in a traditional Asian mortar, made from granite, with a rough, pitted or ridged bowl, which helps to hold the ingredients while they are being pounded with the pestle. Alternatively, for speed, you can use a food processor or blender instead of a mortar and pestle.

Red curry paste

This Thai paste was named after the colour of the chillies used to prepare it. For a hotter paste, add a few chilli seeds.

MAKES ABOUT 175G/6OZ/¾ CUP

5ml/1 tsp coriander seeds, roasted
2.5ml/½ tsp cumin seeds, roasted
12–15 fresh red chillies, seeded and roughly chopped
4 shallots, thinly sliced
2 garlic cloves, chopped
15ml/1 tbsp peeled and chopped fresh galangal
2 lemon grass stalks, chopped
4 fresh coriander roots
10 black peppercorns
good pinch of ground cinnamon
5ml/1 tsp ground turmeric
2.5ml/½ tsp shrimp paste
5ml/1 tsp salt
30ml/2 tbsp vegetable oil

1 Put all the ingredients except the oil in a mortar or food processor and pound or process to a paste.

2 Add the oil, a little at a time, mixing or processing well after each addition. Transfer to a glass jar, and keep in the refrigerator until ready to use.

VARIATIONS

• For Green Curry Paste, process 12–15 green chillies, 2 chopped lemon grass stalks, 3 sliced shallots, 2 garlic cloves, 15ml/1 tbsp chopped galangal, 4 chopped kaffir lime leaves, 2.5ml/½ tsp grated kaffir rind, 5ml/1 tsp each of chopped coriander root, salt, roasted coriander seeds, roasted cumin seeds and shrimp paste, 15ml/1 tbsp granulated sugar, 6 black peppercorns and 15ml/1 tbsp vegetable oil until a paste forms.
• For Yellow Curry Paste, process 6–8 yellow chillies, 1 chopped lemon grass stalk, 4 sliced shallots, 4 garlic cloves, 15ml/1 tbsp chopped fresh root ginger, 5ml/1 tsp coriander seeds, 5ml/1 tsp each of mustard powder and salt, 2.5ml/½ tsp ground cinnamon, 15ml/1 tbsp light brown sugar and 30ml/2 tbsp vegetable oil until a paste forms.

Mussaman curry paste

This hot and spicy paste is used to make the Thai version of a Muslim curry, which is traditionally made with beef, but can also be made with other meats such as chicken or lamb.

MAKES ABOUT 175G/6OZ/¾ CUP

12 large dried red chillies
1 lemon grass stalk
60ml/4 tbsp chopped shallots
5 garlic cloves, roughly chopped
10ml/2 tsp chopped fresh galangal
5ml/1 tsp cumin seeds
15ml/1 tbsp coriander seeds
2 cloves
6 black peppercorns
5ml/1 tsp shrimp paste, prepared
5ml/1 tsp salt
5ml/1 tsp granulated sugar
30ml/2 tbsp vegetable oil

1 Carefully remove the seeds from the dried chillies and discard. Soak the chillies in a bowl of hot water for about 15 minutes.

2 Trim the root end from the lemon grass stalk and slice the lower 5cm/2in of the stalk into small pieces.

3 Place the chopped lemon grass in a dry wok over a low heat, and then add the chopped shallots, garlic and galangal and dry-fry for 2–3 minutes.

4 Stir in the cumin seeds, coriander seeds, cloves and peppercorns and continue to dry-fry over a low heat for 5–6 minutes, stirring constantly. Spoon the mixture into a large mortar.

5 Drain the chillies and add them to the mortar. Grind finely, using the pestle, then add the prepared shrimp paste, salt, sugar and oil and pound again until the mixture forms a rough paste. Use as required, then spoon any leftover paste into a jar, seal tightly and store in the refrigerator for up to 4 months.

COOK'S TIPS

• Preparing a double or larger quantity of paste in a food processor or blender makes the blending of the ingredients easier and the paste will be smoother.
• For the best results, before you start to process the ingredients, slice them up in the following order: galangal, lemon grass, fresh ginger and turmeric, chillies, nuts, shrimp paste, garlic and shallots. Add some of the oil (or coconut cream, if that is to be your frying medium) to the food processor if the mixture is a bit sluggish. If you do this, remember to use less oil or coconut cream when you fry the curry paste to eliminate the raw taste of the ingredients before adding the meat, poultry, fish or vegetables.

PREPARING SHRIMP PASTE

Shrimp paste is a seasoning made from fermented shrimps. It can be bought in Asian food stores. Unless it is to be fried as part of a recipe, it should always be lightly cooked before use.

If you have a gas cooker, simply mould the shrimp paste on to a metal skewer and rotate over a low gas flame, or heat under the grill of an electric cooker, until the outside begins to look crusty but not burnt.

THAILAND, BURMA AND VIETNAM

To eat a Thai meal is an experience in itself, with subtle spice blends and exquisite flavours. Burmese food is more robust yet equally exciting, while Vietnamese cuisine shows the influence of neighbouring China, and there is evidence of traditions left over from French colonial rule.

BURMESE-STYLE PORK CURRY

The cuisine of Burma is influenced by its two neighbours, China and India. Soy sauce and noodles are obviously the result of a Chinese influence, but curry itself is definitely an Indian invention. Burmese curries are, however, much lighter.

SERVES 4–6

2.5cm/1in piece fresh root ginger, crushed
8 dried red chillies, soaked in warm water for 20 minutes
2 lemon grass stalks, finely chopped
15ml/1 tbsp chopped galangal or chopped fresh root ginger
15ml/1 tbsp shrimp paste
30ml/2 tbsp brown sugar
675g/1½lb pork, with some of its fat
600ml/1 pint/2½ cups water
10ml/2 tsp ground turmeric
5ml/1 tsp dark soy sauce
4 shallots, finely chopped
15ml/1 tbsp chopped garlic
45ml/3 tbsp tamarind juice or 5ml/1 tsp concentrated tamarind pulp
5ml/1 tsp granulated sugar
15ml/1 tbsp fish sauce
fresh red chillies, to garnish
French (green) beans, to serve

1 In a mortar, pound the ginger, chillies, lemon grass and galangal into a coarse paste with a pestle, then add the shrimp paste and brown sugar to produce a dark, grainy purée.

2 Cut the pork into large chunks and place in a wok or large pan. Add the curry purée and stir well to make sure the meat is well coated.

3 Cook the pork over a low heat, stirring occasionally, until the meat has changed colour and rendered some of its fat, and the curry paste has begun to release its aroma.

4 Stir the water, turmeric and soy sauce into the meat in the pan. Simmer gently for about 40 minutes, until the meat is tender. The pan does not need to be kept covered.

5 Add the shallots, garlic, tamarind juice, sugar and fish sauce. If you are using concentrated tamarind pulp, stir until dissolved. Garnish with fresh chillies and serve with French beans.

CHICKEN with GINGER and LEMON GRASS

This quick and easy recipe from Vietnam contains the unusual combination of ginger and lemon grass with mandarin orange and chillies. The dish is served topped with peanuts, which are first roasted, then skinned.

SERVES 4–6

3 chicken legs (thighs and drumsticks)
15ml/1 tbsp vegetable oil
2cm/¾in piece fresh root ginger,
    finely chopped
1 garlic clove, crushed
1 small fresh red chilli, seeded and
    finely chopped
5cm/2in piece lemon grass, shredded
150ml/¼ pint/⅔ cup chicken stock
15ml/1 tbsp fish sauce
10ml/2 tsp granulated sugar
2.5ml/½ tsp salt
juice of ½ lemon
50g/2oz raw peanuts
2 spring onions (scallions),
    shredded
zest of 1 mandarin or satsuma,
    shredded
plain boiled rice or rice noodles, to serve

3 To prepare the peanuts, the red skin must be removed. To do this grill (broil) or roast the peanuts under a medium heat until evenly brown, for 2–3 minutes. Turn the nuts out on to a clean cloth and rub briskly to loosen the skins.

4 Transfer the chicken from the pan to a warmed serving dish, and sprinkle with the roasted peanuts, shredded spring onions and the zest of the mandarin or satsuma. Serve hot with plain boiled rice or rice noodles.

1 With the heel of a knife, chop through the narrow end of each of the chicken drumsticks. Remove the jointed parts of the chicken, then remove the skin. Rinse and pat dry with kitchen paper.

2 Heat the oil in a wok or large pan. Add the chicken, ginger, garlic, chilli and lemon grass and cook for 3–4 minutes. Add the chicken stock, fish sauce, sugar, salt and lemon juice. Cover the pan and simmer for 30–35 minutes.

COOK'S TIP
To save yourself time and effort, buy ready-roasted peanuts. These are now available with reduced sodium for a low-salt alternative.

GREEN PAPAYA SALAD

This salad appears in many guises in South-east Asia. If green papaya is not easy to get hold of, finely grated carrots, cucumber or green apple can be used instead. Alternatively, use very thinly sliced white cabbage.

SERVES 4

1 green papaya
4 garlic cloves, roughly chopped
15ml/1 tbsp chopped shallots
3–4 fresh red chillies, seeded and sliced
2.5ml/½ tsp salt
2–3 snake beans or 6 green beans
2 tomatoes, seeded and cut into very
   thin wedges
45ml/3 tbsp Thai fish sauce
15ml/1 tbsp granulated sugar
juice of 1 lime
30ml/2 tbsp coarsely crushed
   roasted peanuts
1 fresh red chilli, seeded and sliced,
   to garnish

1 Cut the papaya in half lengthwise. Scrape out the seeds with a spoon, then peel using a vegetable peeler or a small sharp knife. Shred the flesh finely using a food processor grater.

2 Put the garlic, shallots, chillies and salt in a large mortar and grind to a rough paste with a pestle. Add the shredded papaya, a little at a time, pounding until it becomes slightly limp and soft.

3 Cut the snake beans or green beans into 2cm/¾in lengths. Add the sliced beans and the wedges of tomato to the mortar and crush them very lightly with the pestle.

4 Season the mixture with the Thai fish sauce, sugar and lime juice. Transfer the salad to a serving dish and sprinkle with the crushed peanuts. Garnish with slices of red chilli and serve.

MALAYSIA

The food of Malaysia is a rich blend of some of the world's most exciting cuisines: Malay, Chinese and Indian. The result is a harmonious mixture of flavours, some cool and some famously hot and spicy, such as the dishes cooked in the traditional style known as Nonya.

FRIED FISH with a SPICY SAUCE

Although this is not strictly a curry, it is one of the popular styles of cooking used in Malaysia. Locally known as ikan kecap, *it comes from a small range of Eurasian recipes that combine Western techniques with Eastern flavours.*

SERVES 3–4

450g/1lb fish fillets, such as mackerel, cod or haddock
30ml/2 tbsp plain (all-purpose) flour
groundnut (peanut) oil, for frying
1 onion, roughly chopped
1 small garlic clove, crushed
4cm/1½in piece fresh root ginger, grated
1–2 fresh red chillies, seeded and sliced
1cm/½ in cube shrimp paste, prepared
60ml/4 tbsp water
juice of ½ lemon
15ml/1 tbsp brown sugar
30ml/2 tbsp dark soy sauce
salt
roughly torn lettuce leaves, to serve

1 Rinse the fish fillets under cold water and dry on kitchen paper. Cut into serving portions and remove any bones.

2 Season the flour and use it to dust the fish. Heat some oil and fry the fish on both sides for 3–4 minutes, or until cooked. Transfer to a plate and set aside.

3 Rinse out and dry the pan. Heat a little more oil in the clean frying pan and fry the onion, garlic, ginger and chillies to bring out the flavour. Do not brown.

4 Blend the shrimp paste with the water to make a smooth paste. Add it to the onion mixture, with a little extra water if necessary. Cook for 2 minutes and then stir in the lemon juice, brown sugar and soy sauce.

5 Pour the sauce over the fish and serve, hot or cold, with roughly torn lettuce leaves.

COOK'S TIP
If serving this dish as part of a buffet menu, cut the fish into bitesize pieces.

MALAYSIAN FISH CURRY

The cooking styles of Malaysia have been greatly influenced by neighbouring countries such as India, Indonesia, China and the Middle East. The Malay people thrive on fish curry and rice. This is a superbly flavoured coconut-rich fish curry known as ikan moolee, which is best served with a bowl of steaming hot boiled rice.

SERVES 4

500g/1¼lb monkfish or other
    firm-textured fish fillets, skinned
    and cut into 2.5cm/1in cubes
2.5ml/½ tsp salt
50g/2oz/⅔ cup desiccated (dry,
    unsweetened, shredded) coconut
6 shallots or small onions, chopped
6 blanched almonds
2–3 garlic cloves, roughly chopped
2.5cm/1in piece fresh root ginger, sliced
2 lemon grass stalks, trimmed
10ml/2 tsp ground turmeric
45ml/3 tbsp vegetable oil
2 × 400g/14oz cans coconut milk
1–3 fresh red and green chillies, seeded
    and sliced
salt and ground black pepper, to taste
fresh chives, to garnish
plain boiled rice, to serve

1 Spread out the pieces of fish in a shallow dish and sprinkle them with the salt. Dry-fry the coconut in a wok over a gentle heat, turning all the time until it is crisp and golden (see Cook's Tip).

2 Transfer the coconut to a food processor and process to an oily paste. Scrape into a bowl and reserve.

3 Add the shallots or onions, almonds, garlic and ginger to the food processor. Cut off the lower 5cm/2in of the lemon grass stalks, chop them roughly and add to the processor. Process to a paste.

4 Add the turmeric to the mixture in the food processor and process briefly. Bruise the remaining lemon grass and set the stalks aside.

COOK'S TIP
Dry-frying is a feature of Malay cooking. When dry-frying do not be distracted. The coconut must be constantly on the move so that it becomes crisp and of a uniform golden colour.

5 Heat the oil in a wok. Add the onion mixture and cook for a few minutes without browning. Stir in the coconut milk and bring to the boil, stirring constantly to prevent curdling.

6 Add the cubes of fish to the wok, along with most of the sliced fresh chillies and the bruised lemon grass stalks. Cook for 3–4 minutes. Stir in the coconut paste (this can be moistened with some of the sauce if necessary) and cook for a further 2–3 minutes only. Do not overcook the fish. Taste the curry and adjust the seasoning, as required.

7 Remove the lemon grass. Transfer to a hot serving dish and sprinkle with the remaining slices of chilli. Garnish with chopped and whole chives and serve with plain boiled rice.

CUCUMBER and PINEAPPLE SAMBAL

Sambals are the little side dishes served at almost every Malay meal. In poorer societies,
a main meal may simply be a bowl of rice and a sambal made from pounded shrimp
paste, chillies and lime juice: the sambal is poured over the rice to give it flavour. This
recipe is known as sambal nanas. *Use sparingly, as it is quite fiery.*

SERVES 8–10

1 small or ½ large fresh ripe pineapple
½ cucumber, halved lengthways
50g/2oz dried shrimps
1 large fresh red chilli, seeded
1.25cm/½ in cube shrimp paste, prepared
juice of 1 large lemon or lime
light brown sugar, to taste (optional)
salt

1 Cut off the top and the bottom of the pineapple. Stand it upright on a board, then slice off the skin from top to bottom, cutting out the spines. Slice the pineapple, removing the central core. Cut into thin slices and set aside.

2 Trim the ends from the cucumber and slice thinly. Sprinkle with salt and set aside. Place the dried shrimps in a food processor and chop finely. Add the chilli, prepared shrimp paste and lemon or lime juice, and process again to a paste.

3 Rinse the cucumber, drain and dry on kitchen paper. Mix the pineapple and chill. Just before serving, spoon in the spice mixture with sugar to taste, if liked. Mix well and serve.

COOK'S TIP
The pungent shrimp paste, also called blachan and terasi, is popular in many South-east Asian countries, and is available in Asian food markets. Since it can taste a bit raw in a sambal, dry fry it by wrapping it in foil and heating it in a frying pan over a low heat for 5 minutes, turning from time to time. If the shrimp paste is to be fried with other spices, this preliminary cooking can be eliminated.

INDONESIA

Numerous cultures have flourished among the 13,000 islands of this
lush tropical archipelago, including the Dutch, Portuguese and British.
The result is a rich culinary heritage that makes use of an abundance of
indigenous ingredients, such as rice, chillies, limes, tamarind and spices.

PRAWN CURRY with QUAIL'S EGGS

This exotic combination lives up to all the promises of the East. The earthy flavour of ginger is blended with refreshing lemon grass, fiery red chillies and soothing coconut milk to create this exquisite dish. Quail's eggs are now stocked in most supermarkets.

SERVES 4

12 quail's eggs
30ml/2 tbsp vegetable oil
4 shallots or 1 onion, finely chopped
2.5cm/1in piece fresh galangal or
     2.5cm/1in piece fresh root ginger,
     chopped
2 garlic cloves, crushed
5cm/2in piece lemon grass,
     finely shredded
1–2 small fresh red chillies, seeded and
     finely chopped
2.5ml/½ tsp ground turmeric
12mm/½in cube shrimp paste or
     15ml/1 tbsp fish sauce
900g/2lb raw prawn (shrimp) tails,
     peeled and deveined
400g/14oz can coconut milk
300ml/½ pint/1¼ cups chicken stock
115g/4oz Chinese leaves,
     roughly shredded
10ml/2 tsp granulated sugar
2.5ml/½ tsp salt
2 spring onions (scallions), green part
     only, shredded, and 30ml/2 tbsp
     shredded coconut, to garnish

1 Boil the quail's eggs for 8 minutes. Refresh in cold water, peel by dipping in cold water to release the shells and set them aside.

2 Heat the vegetable oil in a large wok, add the shallots or onion, galangal or ginger and garlic and cook until the onions have softened, without colouring. Add the lemon grass, chillies, turmeric and shrimp paste or fish sauce and fry briefly to bring out their flavours.

3 Add the prawns to the wok and fry briefly. Pour the coconut milk through a sieve (strainer) over a bowl, then add the thin part of the milk with the chicken stock. Add the Chinese leaves, sugar and salt, and bring to the boil. Simmer for 6–8 minutes.

4 Turn out the prawn curry on to a warmed serving dish. Halve the quail's eggs, using a sharp knife for a clean cut, and toss them in the sauce until they are well coated. Sprinkle with the spring onions and the shredded coconut. Serve with plain boiled rice, if you like.

SQUID in CLOVE SAUCE

The island of Madura, between Bali and Java, makes use of various spices that were originally introduced to Indonesia by Indian and Arab traders. This recipe with cloves and nutmeg, along with tomato and soy sauce, is known as Cumi Cumi Smoor. It is quite delicious, and not difficult to make.

SERVES 3–4

675g/1½lb ready-cleaned squid
45ml/3 tbsp groundnut (peanut) oil
1 onion, finely chopped
2 garlic cloves, crushed
1 beefsteak tomato, skinned and chopped
15ml/1 tbsp dark soy sauce
2.5ml/½ tsp grated nutmeg
6 whole cloves
150ml/¼ pint/⅔ cup water
juice of ½ lemon or lime
salt and ground black pepper, to taste
shredded spring onions (scallions) and fresh
    coriander (cilantro) sprigs, to garnish
plain boiled rice, to serve

1 Wash the squid and pat dry on kitchen paper. Use a sharp kitchen knife to cut the squid into long, thin ribbons. Carefully remove the "bone" from each tentacle, and discard.

2 Heat a wok, toss in the squid and stir constantly for 2–3 minutes, when the squid will have curled into attractive shapes or into firm rings. Lift out and set aside in a warm place.

3 Heat the oil in a clean pan and fry the onion and garlic, until soft and beginning to brown. Add the tomato, soy sauce, nutmeg, cloves, water and lemon or lime juice. Bring to the boil and then reduce the heat and add the squid, with seasoning to taste.

4 Cook the squid in the sauce for 3–5 minutes, uncovered, over a gentle heat, stirring from time to time. Take care not to overcook the squid. Serve hot or warm, with plain rice, or as part of a buffet spread. Garnish with shredded spring onions and fresh coriander.

VARIATION
Instead of squid try using 450g/1lb cooked and peeled tiger prawns (shrimp) in this recipe. Add them to the pan for the final 1–2 minutes.

FRUIT and RAW VEGETABLE GADO-GADO

Banana leaves, which can be bought from Asian markets, lend an authentic touch to all types of South-east Asian dishes. They are most frequently used as wrappers in which to cook small parcels of food, but if you are serving this salad for a special occasion, you could use a single banana leaf instead of the mixed salad leaves to line the platter.

SERVES 6

½ cucumber
2 pears (not too ripe) or 175g/6oz wedge
    of yam bean
1–2 eating apples
juice of ½ lemon
mixed salad leaves or 1–2 banana leaves
6 tomatoes, seeded and cut into wedges
3 fresh pineapple slices, cored and cut
    into wedges
3 eggs, hard-boiled (hard-cooked) and
    shelled
175g/6oz egg noodles, cooked, cooled
    and chopped
Deep-fried Onions, to garnish

For the peanut sauce
2–4 fresh red chillies, seeded and ground,
    or 15ml/1 tbsp Hot Tomato Sambal
300ml/½ pint/1¼ cups coconut milk
350g/12oz/1¼ cups crunchy peanut butter
15ml/1 tbsp dark soy sauce or dark brown
    sugar
5ml/1 tsp tamarind pulp, soaked in 45ml/
    3 tbsp warm water
coarsely crushed peanuts
salt

VARIATION
Quail's eggs can be used in place of hen's
eggs. Hard boil for 3 minutes.

1 Make the peanut sauce. Put the ground chillies or Hot Tomato Sambal in a pan. Pour in the coconut milk, then stir in the peanut butter. Heat gently, stirring, until well blended.

2 Simmer gently until the sauce thickens, then stir in the soy sauce or sugar. Strain in the tamarind juice, add salt to taste and stir well. Spoon into a bowl and sprinkle with coarsely crushed peanuts.

3 To make the salad, core the cucumber and peel the pears or yam bean. Cut the flesh into fine matchsticks. Finely shred the apples and sprinkle them with the lemon juice. Spread a bed of mixed salad leaves on a flat platter and pile the cucumber, pear or yam bean, apple, tomato and pineapple on top.

4 Add the sliced or quartered hard-boiled eggs, the chopped noodles and garnish with the Deep-fried Onions. Serve the salad at once, with the peanut sauce.

SAMBAL KECAP, HOT TOMATO SAMBAL and CUCUMBER SAMBAL

Piquant sambals are placed on the table as a condiment for dipping meat and fish.

SAMBAL KECAP

MAKES ABOUT 150ML/¼ PINT/⅔ CUP

1 fresh red chilli, seeded and
    finely chopped
2 garlic cloves, crushed
60ml/4 tbsp dark soy sauce
20ml/4 tsp lemon juice, or
    15–25ml/1–1½ tbsp prepared tamarind
    juice or 5ml/1 tsp concentrated
    tamarind pulp
30ml/2 tbsp hot water
30ml/2 tbsp Deep-fried Onions

1 Mix the chilli, garlic, soy sauce, lemon
juice or tamarind juice or pulp and hot
water together in a bowl.

2 Stir in the Deep-fried Onions and
then leave the sambal to stand for
30 minutes before serving.

HOT TOMATO SAMBAL

MAKES 120ML/4FL OZ/½ CUP

3 ripe tomatoes
2.5ml/½ tsp salt
5ml/1 tsp chilli sauce
60ml/4 tbsp fish sauce or soy sauce
15ml/1 tbsp chopped fresh coriander
    (cilantro) leaves

1 Cover the tomatoes with boiling
water to loosen the skins. Remove the
skins, halve, discard the seeds and chop
the flesh finely.

2 Place the chopped tomatoes in a large
bowl, add the salt, chilli sauce, fish sauce
or soy sauce and chopped coriander

3 Mix together well. Leave the sambal
to stand for 30 minutes before serving.

CUCUMBER SAMBAL

MAKES 150ML/5FL OZ/⅔ CUP

1 clove garlic, crushed
5ml/1 tsp fennel seeds
10ml/2 tsp granulated sugar
2.5ml/½ tsp salt
2 shallots or 1 small onion, finely sliced
100ml/4fl oz/½ cup rice or white wine
    vinegar
¼ cucumber, finely diced

1 Place the garlic, fennel seeds, sugar
and salt in a pestle and mortar and
pound finely. Alternatively, grind the
ingredients thoroughly in a food
processor.

2 Stir in the shallots or onion, vinegar
and cucumber. Leave to stand for 6–8
hours to allow the flavours to combine.

COCONUT and PEANUT RELISH and HOT CHILLI AND GARLIC DIPPING SAUCE

These flavoursome accompaniments can be served with many Indonesian dishes.

COCONUT AND PEANUT RELISH

MAKES 120ML/4FL OZ/½ CUP

115g/4oz fresh coconut, grated,
   or desiccated (dry, unsweetened,
   shredded) coconut
175g/6oz/1 cup salted peanuts
5mm/¼in cube shrimp paste
1 small onion, quartered
2–3 garlic cloves, crushed
45ml/3 tbsp vegetable oil
2.5ml/½ tsp tamarind pulp, soaked in
   30ml/2 tbsp warm water
5ml/1 tsp coriander seeds, roasted
   and ground
2.5ml/½ tsp cumin seeds, roasted
   and ground
5ml/1 tsp dark brown sugar

1 Dry-fry the coconut in a wok or large pan over a medium heat, stirring the coconut constantly until crisp and golden colour. Allow to cool and add half to the peanuts in a bowl. Toss together to mix.

2 Process the shrimp paste, the onion and garlic in a food processor or with a pestle and mortar to form a paste. Fry the paste in hot oil, without browning.

3 Strain the tamarind and reserve the juice. Add the coriander, cumin, tamarind juice and brown sugar to the fried paste in the pan. Cook for 3 minutes, stirring.

4 Stir in the remaining toasted coconut and leave to cool. When cold, mix with the peanut and coconut mixture. Leave to stand for 30 minutes before serving.

HOT CHILLI AND GARLIC DIPPING SAUCE

MAKES 120ML/4FL OZ/½ CUP

1 garlic clove
2 fresh Thai red chillies, seeded and
   roughly chopped
10ml/2 tsp granulated sugar
5ml/1 tsp tamarind juice
60ml/4 tbsp soy sauce
juice of ½ lime

1 Process the garlic, chillies and sugar in a food processor or with a pestle and mortar to create a smooth paste.

2 Add the tamarind juice, soy sauce and lime juice, and mix together. Leave to stand for 30 minutes before serving.

THE PHILIPPINES

Filipino cuisine shows the influence of neighbouring China, Malaysia, Japan and Indonesia, but by far the strongest influence came from the Spanish settlers who arrived to colonize the islands in the 16th century, and stayed for nearly 400 years.

MIXED MEAT SOUP

A Filipino pot-au-feu with Spanish connections, this dish is known as Puchero. Sometimes it is served as two courses, first soup, then meat and vegetables with rice, but it can happily be served as is, on rice in a wide soup bowl. Either way it is very satisfying, and a siesta afterwards is highly recommended.

SERVES 6–8

225g/8oz/generous 1 cup chickpeas,
   soaked overnight in water to cover
1.3kg/3lb chicken, cut into 8 pieces
350g/12oz belly of pork, rinded, or pork
   fillet, cubed
2 chorizo, thickly sliced
2 onions, chopped
2.5 litres/4 pints/10 cups water
60ml/4 tbsp vegetable oil
2 garlic cloves, crushed
3 large tomatoes, peeled, seeded
   and chopped
15ml/1 tbsp tomato purée (paste)
1–2 sweet potatoes, cut into 1cm/
   ½in cubes
2 plantains or unripe bananas,
   sliced (optional)
salt and ground black pepper
chives or chopped spring onions
   (scallions), to garnish
½ head Chinese leaves (Chinese cabbage),
   shredded, to serve

For the aubergine sauce
1 large aubergine (eggplant)
3 garlic cloves, crushed
60–90ml/4–6 tbsp wine or cider vinegar

1 Drain the chickpeas and put them in a pan. Cover with water, bring to the boil and boil rapidly for 10 minutes. Reduce the heat and simmer for 30 minutes until the chickpeas are half tender. Drain.

2 Put the chicken pieces, pork, chorizo and half of the onions in a pan. Add the chickpeas and pour in the water. Bring to the boil and lower the heat, cover and simmer for 1 hour or until the meat is just tender when tested with a skewer.

3 Meanwhile, make the aubergine sauce. Preheat the oven to 200°C/400°F/Gas 6. Prick the aubergine in several places, then place it on a baking sheet and bake for 30 minutes or until very soft.

4 Cool slightly, then peel away the aubergine skin and scrape the flesh into a bowl. Mash the flesh with the crushed garlic, season to taste and add enough vinegar to sharpen the sauce, which should be quite piquant. Set aside.

5 Heat the oil in a wok or large pan and fry the remaining onion and garlic for 5 minutes, until soft but not brown. Add the tomatoes and tomato purée and cook for 2 minutes, then add this mixture to a pan with the diced sweet potato. Add the plantains or unripe bananas, if using. Cook over a gentle heat for 20 minutes until the sweet potato is cooked. Add the Chinese leaves for the last minute or two.

6 Spoon the thick meat soup into a soup tureen, and put the vegetables in a separate serving bowl. Garnish both with whole or chopped chives or spring onions and serve with Chinese leaves and the aubergine sauce. Plain boiled rice goes very well with this dish.

INDONESIAN FRIED RICE

One of the most familiar and well-known Indonesian dishes, Nasi Goreng is a marvellous
way to use up leftover rice, chicken and meats such as pork. It is important that the rice
is quite cold and the grains are separate before adding the other ingredients.

SERVES 4–6

350g/12oz/¾ cups dry weight long grain
    rice, such as basmati, cooked and
    allowed to become completely cold
2 eggs
30ml/2 tbsp water
105ml/7 tbsp vegetable oil
225g/8oz pork fillet or fillet of beef
115g/4oz peeled, cooked prawns (shrimp)
175–225g/6–8oz cooked chicken, chopped
2–3 fresh red chillies, seeded and sliced
1cm/½in cube shrimp paste
2 garlic cloves, crushed
1 onion, sliced
30ml/2 tbsp dark soy sauce or
    45–60ml/3–4 tbsp tomato ketchup
salt and ground black pepper
celery leaves, fresh coriander (cilantro)
    sprigs, to garnish

1 Once the rice is cooked and cooled,
fork it through to separate the grains
and keep it in a covered pan or dish
until required.

2 Beat the eggs with seasoning and the
water and make two or three omelettes
in a frying pan, with a minimum of oil.
Roll up each omelette and cut into strips
when cold. Set aside.

3 Cut the pork or beef into neat strips
and put the meat, prawns and chicken
pieces in separate bowls. Shred one of
the chillies and reserve it.

COOK'S TIP
Always store cooked and cooled rice in
the refrigerator.

4 Put the shrimp paste, with the
remaining chilli, garlic and onion, in a
food processor and grind to a paste, or
pound using a pestle and mortar.

5 Fry the paste in the remaining hot oil,
without browning, until it gives off a rich,
spicy aroma. Add the strips of pork or
beef and fry over a high heat to seal in
the juices. Stir constantly to prevent the
meat sticking to the bottom of the pan.

6 Add the prawns, cook for 2 minutes
and then stir in the chicken, cold rice,
dark soy sauce or ketchup and seasoning
to taste. Stir constantly to keep the rice
light and fluffy and prevent it from
sticking to the base of the pan.

7 Turn on to a hot platter and garnish
with the omelette strips, celery leaves,
reserved shredded fresh chilli and
coriander sprigs.

PINEAPPLE FRIED RICE

When buying a pineapple, look for a sweet-smelling fruit with an even brownish/yellow skin. To test for ripeness, tap the base – a dull sound indicates that the fruit is ripe. The flesh should also give slightly when pressed.

SERVES 4–6

I pineapple
30ml/2 tbsp vegetable oil
I small onion, finely chopped
2 fresh green chillies, seeded and chopped
225g/8oz lean pork, cut into strips
115g/4oz cooked, peeled prawns (shrimp)
675–900g/1½–2lb/3–4 cups plain boiled
    rice, cooked and completely cold
50g/2oz/⅓ cup roasted cashew nuts
2 spring onions (scallions), chopped
30ml/2 tbsp fish sauce
15ml/1 tbsp soy sauce
2 fresh red chillies, sliced, and 10–12 fresh
    mint leaves (optional), to garnish

1 Using a sharp knife, cut the pineapple into quarters. Remove the flesh from both halves by cutting around inside the skin. Reserve the pineapple skin shells for serving the rice.

2 Slice the pineapple flesh and chop it into small even-size cubes. You will need about 115g/4oz of pineapple in total. Any remaining fruit can be reserved for use in a dessert.

3 Heat the oil in a wok or large pan. Add the onion and chillies and fry for about 3–5 minutes until softened. Add the strips of pork and cook until they have browned on all sides.

4 Stir in the prawns and rice and toss well together. Continue to stir-fry until the rice is thoroughly heated.

5 Add the chopped pineapple, cashew nuts and spring onions. Season to taste with fish sauce and soy sauce.

6 Spoon into the pineapple skin shells. Garnish with sliced red chillies, and with shredded mint leaves, if you like.

COOK'S TIP
This dish is ideal to prepare for a special occasion meal. Served in the pineapple skin shells, it is sure to be the talking point of the dinner.

THAI FRIED NOODLES

Phat Thai, as this dish is known, has a fascinating flavour and texture. It is made with rice noodles, combined with shellfish and beancurd, a range of vegetables and ground peanuts, and is considered one of the national dishes of Thailand.

SERVES 4–6

350g/12oz rice noodles
45ml/3 tbsp vegetable oil
15ml/1 tbsp chopped garlic
16 raw king prawns (jumbo shrimp),
    peeled, tails left intact and deveined
2 eggs, lightly beaten
15ml/1 tbsp dried shrimps, rinsed
30ml/2 tbsp pickled white radish
50g/2oz fried beancurd or tofu, chopped
2.5ml/½ tsp dried chilli flakes
115g/4oz garlic chives, cut into 5cm/
    2in lengths
225g/8oz/1 cup beansprouts
50g/2oz/⅓ cup roasted peanuts,
    coarsely ground
5ml/1 tsp granulated sugar
15ml/1 tbsp dark soy sauce
30ml/2 tbsp fish sauce
30ml/2 tbsp tamarind juice or 5ml/1 tsp
    concentrated tamarind pulp
30ml/2 tbsp fresh coriander (cilantro)
    leaves and 1 kaffir lime, to garnish

1 Soak the noodles in a bowl of warm water for 20–30 minutes, then drain.

2 Heat 15ml/1 tbsp of the oil in a wok or large pan. Add the garlic and fry until golden. Stir in the prawns and cook for 1–2 minutes until pink, tossing from time to time. Remove and set aside.

3 Heat another 15ml/1 tbsp of oil in the pan. Add the eggs and tilt the wok to spread them into a thin sheet. Stir to scramble and break the egg into small pieces. Remove from the pan and set aside with the prawns.

4 Heat the remaining oil in the same pan. Add the dried shrimps, pickled radish, beancurd or tofu and dried chillies. Stir-fry briefly. Add the soaked noodles and stir-fry for 5 minutes.

5 Add the garlic chives, half the beansprouts and half the peanuts. Season with the granulated sugar, soy sauce, fish sauce and tamarind juice or pulp. Mix well and cook until the noodles are completely heated through.

6 Return the prawn and egg mixture to the pan and mix with the noodles. Serve garnished with the rest of the beansprouts, peanuts, coriander leaves and kaffir lime wedges, if using.

COOK'S TIP
Pickled white radish is available in jars from Asian food stores and markets.

PICTURE CREDITS
Additional picture material
supplied by Life File:
page 10, page 11 top, page
12, page 13 top and bottom,
p167 top right, p168, 169
top and bottom, page 170,
page 171 top and bottom.